has taught over 30 years in our prestigious technical leadership pro-
is one of our top instructors. He is masterful at simplifying com-
oject management problems and easily translating them for
nals to apply. I have witnessed thousands of business and technol-
ers who have applied the principles of his book to excel in projects."

—**Joon Lee**, Program Manager, UCLA Extension Technical
Management Program

book has served as a blueprint for implementing change in our
organization and establishing our very first PMO. His simple and
approach made it possible for our managers to begin thinking and
trategically to accomplish our most important goals."

Sheppard, Director of Business Systems & Project Management,
The Navigators

love this methodology and are actively applying these concepts
and programs that improve national security. This approach
egy simple, practical, and actionable. I recommend this to any
faces big challenges and wants to make a greater impact."

mmy P. Taylor, Ph.D, former Chief Operating Officer, National
Security Directorate, Pacific Northwest National Laboratory

k has added another dimension to my understanding of strategy
management. This is an essential guide for every project man-
ecutive, and every leader."

orovyak, Project Director, Immunovant, host of WITS podcast
What It Takes to Succeed

eams and projects, read this book! Too many books complicate
delivering results. Terry does a masterful job of laying out prac-
can simplify your ability to get strategic projects delivered."

fman, Project Management and Leadership Keynote Speaker,
Author, Coach, and Podcast Host

and life experience add a dimension to this topic not usually
ess strategy books. Not only does he offer a simple and effec-
planning and achieving results, but he also recognizes that
's self-mastery skill set plays a huge role in leading teams to
This is a very human book."

Susan S. Radwan, President of the Association for Strategic
Planning 2021–2022

Praise for *Strategic Project Manage...*
Second Edition

"A much stronger focus on implementation
change-driven world, where most fundamental
been disrupted. Terry's book is the perfect g
organization navigate through this new reality

　　—**Antonio Nieto-Rodriguez**, former G
　　Management Institute, Strategy Imple

"This is the book to read if you are serious ab
a strategic perspective. I have hundreds of pr
personal reference library, and this one quid
list. Bottom line: Terry may well have creat
the test of time!"

　　—**Lee R. Lambert**, a founder of the

"Terry has made a valuable contribution t
with this second edition. Today's project l
approach to enable project management
and change."

　　—**Jesús Martínez-Almela**, for

"This book reveals what may be the
ment. I love how it connects the strat
and bolts of execution in a clear, con
case should include a Logical Frame
missing link in project design."

　　—**Eric Verzuh**, author, *The Fast-F*

"This book is a fantastic resource
control of their projects' strategy ar
guide executives on the critical qu
projects—highly recommended!"

　　—**Hassan Osman**, PMO

"Terry
gram ar
plex pr
professi
ogy lead

"Terry's
nonprofit
accessible
planning
　　—**David**

"My teams
to projects
makes stra
leader who
　　—**Ta**

"Terry's boo
and project
ager, every e
　　—**Igor Zd**

"If you lead t
the process of
tical tools that
　　—**Andy Kau**

"Terry's humo
found in busin
tive approach t
a project leade
project success.

"Great project management is the 'superpower' that turns vision into reality, but it is rarely taught well, if at all. Terry's book is a refreshing return to common sense, providing simple tools and a common language to help teams increase their impact."

—**Deepa Prahalad**, Design Strategist, Coauthor, *Predictable Magic*, Thinkers50 India

"Terry's book is the definitive guide on turning strategy into action! His simple and practical system allows managers to develop effective project plans for their organizations more easily."

—**Anne Kurzrock**, Regional Director of Chicago and Virtual Programs, The Institute for Management Studies

"Whether you are an executive, project manager, or supervisor, leading change is central to your success. If you want to learn how, follow Terry's strategic project management approach to energize your key initiatives and achieve successful and sustainable change."

—**Barbara Trautlein, Ph.D**, Author of Change Intelligence and Chief Catalyst at Change Catalysts, LLC

"I have used Terry's system to build my business and career to a level of success I could not have imagined. Give it a try and discover what innovative project strategy can do for you."

—**Joseph McClendon III**, Ultimate Performance Specialist

"Terry's book provided the basis upon which MIT developed an approach to strategic project planning and design in research and development. This approach is now part of our Chemical Engineering Projects Laboratory. It has demonstrably improved the performance of graduate student teams and taught them critical skills early in their training."

—**Clark K. Colton, Ph.D**, Professor of Chemical Engineering, Massachusetts Institute of Technology

"This book delivers what it promises—a process and a framework to better align projects to organization strategy. Terry's process and framework helps organizations better select and justify projects that are 'strategy relevant.' This edition features interesting stories and simple concepts that anyone can implement in any organization. The book also deals with the preparation needed to build effective teams . . . welcome additions that are missing from most project management books."

—**Howard Rohm**, Cofounder and President, Balanced Scorecard Institute

"I love applying Terry's Logical Framework at home and at work because it allows me to remove the clutter and organize my thoughts in a way to reach the desired outcomes. At work, it has helped me pull together differing opinions, get the team on the same page, ferret out erroneous assumptions, and develop a cohesive path forward."

—**Jordan Blasdel Vannoy**, Executive Director of Human Resources and Organizational Development, Princeton Plasma Physics Laboratory

"Terry is a tremendous thinker and passionate teacher. He writes in a way that takes complex issues and explains them in very understandable and executable ways. These days everyone needs the powerful strategies that he shares in this book."

—**Chris Coffey**, President, Marshall Goldsmith Stakeholder Centered Coaching®

"Terry's strategic thinking and action approach has done wonders in my life and I believe that every leader needs to have their teams read this golden nugget. Terry's logical framework approach will transform the way you think about leading complex initiatives and even your life in general. Projects using his approach have been highlighted as the best IT showcased projects at different companies."

—**Pooja Sund**, Director of Engineering Finance, Microsoft

"The simple system in this book has enabled me to quickly align our teams around what we are trying to achieve and to measure success at every level. I first used the method to pivot a component manufacturer toward electromechanical assembly, which allowed us to grow from $40 million to over $120 million in revenue. This is the number-one tool in my toolbox to align the organization, develop KPIs, and establish risk control plans."

—**Fernando Amaro**, Industrial Entrepreneur

"Terry's second edition builds on the strengths of his first edition with rich insights for bridging the gap between organizational strategies and project execution. In an era that increasingly requires organizations to link projects and programs to business strategies, Terry offers actionable and effective ways to increase performance and organizational success through projects."

—**Stacy Goff**, CEO, ProjectExperts, IPMA Honorary Fellow

"Learn from a master as Terry offers practical hands-on tools for tackling the tough issues that keep good leaders awake at night. Terry takes you from the surreal to the real world of strategic thinking and planning."

—**James Whalen**, Vice President, DirecTV, Inc.

"Terry's book is the Swiss Army knife for delivering a successful initiative. Whether using Agile or other methods, I now begin with Terry's Framework and the Four Fundamental Questions to ensure that my business initiatives are designed for success. This book sets itself apart from other project management books by offering an easy-to-follow path to guide us from idea to the promised results. A project management home run!"

—**Till Hollmann**, Vice President/General Manager, Crane
ChemPharma & Energy

"One reason some startups turn into successful businesses is that the entrepreneur uses a proven system to turn their good ideas into a strategy they can implement. Terry's book lays out the process of turning strategy into action in great detail, based on years of studying both failure and success. Every businessperson can benefit from his wisdom."

—**Robert Youker**, Senior Project Management Instructor, World Bank
(retired), cofounder of the Project Management Institute

"Project management software can be a headache because it's usually hard to learn and teaches you how to track projects rather than how to manage them. Terry's book is the pain reliever for these headaches because he helps you understand project management, so you learn it easily and quickly, and apply it successfully."

—**Jim McComb**, past President, Association for Strategic Planning, and
author, *Certain Success in an Uncertain World*

"This book is the ultimate tool for any PM who wants to minimize frustration, motivate his staff, and deliver the goods far beyond those of mortal project managers."

—**Hendrie Weisinger**, Psychologist and Author,
Performing Under Pressure

"I have used Terry's book in the MBA program I teach at Golden Gate University and found it an ideal tool for students who are learning about strategic analysis and design. There are some books that every professional should read, apply, and keep on their bookshelf for ready reference. This is one of them."

—**Mary Anne Brady, Ph.D**, University Instructor and Strategy Consultant

"This book offers a clear-cut explanation of how the various goals and objectives of a project relate to each other, and this motivates project managers to go that extra mile to ensure success. My department is using this breakthrough approach for projects designed to help integrate refugees and immigrants into communities in Europe."

—**Ali Rashidi**, Director, Department for International Cooperation, Folkuniversitetet Uppsala Sweden

"Terry's methodology has been a guide that I have personally used to plan various strategic initiatives. I have since tried other methodologies, but I find myself referring back to his framework, which is simple and can help anyone break down major issues into manageable components to achieve results."

—**Jimmy Godard**, International Leadership Speaker and past President, PMI Portland Chapter

"This is a must-read for professionals of all ages. Terry is uniquely gifted in that his writing is transformative. When you read it, you feel as if he is in the room with you and truly cares about your professional and personal development. You will be provoked, stretched, inspired, and equipped to deploy your best self!"

—**Chip Espinoza, Ph.D**, Author, *Managing the Millennials*

"This approach is as indispensable as it is simple. My project teams use it when we develop cybersecurity solutions for our clients. It keeps us on track and helps us reduce risks and faulty assumptions that cause projects to fail."

—**David Lam**, former *Los Angeles Business Journal* Nonprofit CIO of the Year

"Strategic thinking is often missed in project management, causing a wide range of issues and problems. Terry's framework is an extremely helpful guide on how to bridge this gap and create effective change. No matter the size and type of your project, I highly recommend this to anyone interested in successful transformation."

—**Rikke Wend Hartung**, Business Transformation Consultant, and Project Manager, Denmark

"The benefits of planning with Terry's approach are crystal clear."

—**Adam Gilmore**, Space Station Mechanisms Lead, NASA

"Terry's system is simple and practical for use in work and in life. I use this with my work team to improve productivity and to plan my career and family future."

—**Wanchai Sri-Isaraporn**, General Manager, Toyota Motor Thailand Co., Ltd.

"Terry's framework is very effective for linking corporate goals to business unit targets and individual outcomes."

—**Patchara Thanattrai,** Vice President, Human Resources, The Stock Exchange of Thailand

"Terry provides a clear and compelling methodology for creating enterprise-wide strategies that integrate all of our sub-departments. This is a must-read book for any leader who wants to revitalize their organization."

—**Dale Hough**, Chief of Reengineering, Los Angeles County Assessor's Office

"As an engineer, I'm reluctant to get all weepy about management processes, but Terry's model is a logical and demonstrably effective tool for organizing and executing complex strategies."

—**David Sanders**, Engineer, TRW

"Hits the nail on the head with fresh approaches to design and implements projects that achieve their goals."

—**Philippe Goetschel**, Director (retired), Microsoft Corporation

"Lots of management tools sound good in theory but are hard to apply. Terry provides a practical planning breakthrough that has helped our team to start faster, think smarter, and get more done."

—**Lynn Ballard**, IT Security Manager, Beckman Coulter

"This book provides concise, simple, and highly effective tools to turn problems into action plans. No project is too complex when broken down using Terry's four strategic questions and the Logical Framework tool."

—**Anne Wu**, Lean Six Sigma Black Belt, 3M Unitek

"Terry changed how I do my planning and this has significantly increased my ability to reach my goals."

—**Laurie Triplett**, environmental physicist, Los Alamos National Laboratory

"These tools will not only benefit you but will benefit your whole team."
—**Kumar Talinki**, Senior Software Engineer, Symantec Corporation

"Makes it much easier to visualize complex and large projects. This helps you to effectively communicate and present your ideas to the whole team."
—**Keith Bonnici**, Program Manager, TEKES, Finland

"This approach gave our planners, managers, and analysts the tools and insight to successfully redirect a major process reengineering effort taking place in a rapidly changing IT landscape."
—**Michael J. Greenhalgh**, Supervisor, Sacramento Municipal Utility District

"Strategic management can be a very dry subject. However, true masters can turn this dry topic into a most enlightening and highly usable management tool. Terry is one such rare master. You would be wise to read his book and even wiser to attend his course."
—**Regent B.H. Khor**, Senior Marketing Officer, JTC Corporation, Government of Singapore

STRATEGIC
PROJECT
MANAGEMENT
MADE SIMPLE

STRATEGIC PROJECT MANAGEMENT MADE SIMPLE

SOLUTION TOOLS FOR LEADERS
AND TEAMS

Second Edition

TERRY DEAN SCHMIDT

WILEY

Published by John Wiley & Sons, Inc., Hoboken, New Jersey.
Published simultaneously in Canada.

For general information on our other products and services or for technical support, please contact our Customer Care Department within the United States at (800) 762-2974, outside the United States at (317) 572-3993 or fax (317) 572-4002.

Wiley publishes in a variety of print and electronic formats and by print-on-demand. Some material included with standard print versions of this book may not be included in e-books or in print-on-demand. If this book refers to media such as a CD or DVD that is not included in the version you purchased, you may download this material at http://booksupport.wiley.com. For more information about Wiley products, visit www.wiley.com.

Library of Congress Cataloging-in-Publication Data:

Names: Schmidt, Terry, author.
Title: Strategic project management made simple : solution tools for
  leaders and teams / Terry Schmidt.
Description: Second edition. | Hoboken, New Jersey : Wiley, [2021] |
  Includes index.
Identifiers: LCCN 2021008514 (print) | LCCN 2021008515 (ebook) | ISBN
  9781119718178 (hardback) | ISBN 9781119718185 (adobe pdf) | ISBN
  9781119718154 (epub)
Subjects: LCSH: Project management. | Strategic planning.
Classification: LCC HD69.P75 S363 2021 (print) | LCC HD69.P75 (ebook) |
  DDC 658.4/012—dc23
LC record available at https://lccn.loc.gov/2021008514
LC ebook record available at https://lccn.loc.gov/2021008515

Cover image: © ssstep / Getty Images
Cover design: Wiley

SKY10025824_032421

To every person who is committed to making the world a better place by learning and applying simple strategies to enhance their work and life.

That's been one of my mantras—focus and simplicity. Simple can be harder than complex: You have to work hard to get your thinking clean to make it simple. But it's worth it in the end because once you get there, you can move mountains.

—Steve Jobs

Contents

PART II:
Mastering the Four Critical
Strategic Questions

Acknowledgments

Writing a book is never a solitary project. I am grateful to the many people who contributed to my learning journey and made this book possible.

Thanks to the leadership team of the UCLA Extension Technical Management Program: Program Manager Joon Lee, Dr. Bill Goodin, Dr. Varaz Shamirian, Mazen Khawaja, and Gina Springer. You gave me freedom to innovate in my courses. And to my fellow instructors, you made it fun.

My colleagues from the Association for Strategic Planning enriched my insights, especially Alan Leeds, Joyce Reynolds-Sinclair, Jim McComb, Lee Crumbaugh, Jim Stockmal, Howard Rohm, Randy Rollinson, Marie Muscella, Denise McNerney, and Sue Radawan. Harvard Business School classmate Michael Porter added immensely to my understanding of strategy.

My learning was enhanced in working with my global partners at the Haines Centre for Strategic Management, especially Valerie MacLeod, Stephen Lin, Gail Aller-Stead, Gerald Taylor, Barbara Collins, Jim McKinley, Sheri Barker, Loren Tarantino, Alan Bandt, Lewe Atkinson, and the late Stephen Haines.

I'm grateful for the support and trust of Chad Barr, Donald van Stone, Fernando Amaro, Cheryl Schmidt, Dan Barr, Ashley Guberman, Molly Hageboeck, Keith Russell, Abdirahman Guleid and Lori Heiner, amazing people who provided encouraging words just when I needed them most. Dr. Hendrie Weisinger inspired creative thinking in his unique way.

My crackerjack peer review team provided insights to enrich my own. Patti Lowe was there from the very start and added value through her dedicated commitment to make the world better. Bob Hessler breathed dull paragraphs to life and created smoother idea flow.

Tim McClintock, Till Hollman, and David Paul brought their high-level industry expertise to this project. Leanna Blackmon went the extra mile in helping to meet the final deadline, just as she did in the first edition. Michael Beaton pitched in with his wide-ranging perspective and provocative questions. Art Drexler made the graphics sparkle.

Also pitching in along the way were Vanessa Bryant, Glenn Hamamura, Michael Fraidenburg, Geri Dennison, Marcelene Anderson, Jim Roberts, Patty Neil, Siarhei Tuzik, Lori Nevin, Sue Schwede, Stephen Lin, Farooq Omar, and Ann Tarasena.

The hardest-working member of my team was Kavitha Jain, who deciphered my scribbles and typed an endless stream of messy revisions without complaint. I could not have done it without her.

The Institute of Management Studies has been supportive over the past three decades. My appreciation goes to Charles Good, Jon and Lisa Peters, Anne Kurzrock, and Karla Peters-Van Havel, and to the chairpersons of all the IMS regions that hosted my seminars.

My many friends in the global project management community continue to share their wisdom and enhance my own in the process.

Thanks also to MIT professor Clark Colton, who invited me to teach Emotional Intelligence for teams at the MIT Professional Institute.

My outstanding literary agent Jeff Herman found the ideal publisher for this project. It was a privilege working with the pros at John Wiley & Sons: Shannon Vargo, Deborah Schindlar, Sally Davis, Kelly Langford, Selvakumaran Rajendiran and the team at Cape Cod Compositors.

My deepest appreciation goes to the many clients in business and government that I have been privileged to serve. You were not only my clients; you were my friends. By rolling up our sleeves and solving real problems together, we make a difference where it really matters.

Writing a book can be a long and lonely process but my wonderful wife Sinee—44 years and counting—tolerated my mood swings and cheered me up when I got stuck. My super dog Rufus, a loving and shy rescue Shih Tzu, snuggled under my desk and kept my toes warm during many long nights of writing, rewriting, polishing, and (finally) completing.

You all played a role in bringing to life a book that will empower leaders of all types to make a greater difference. Thank you all so much for making this contribution to strategic management excellence possible!

Introduction

Projects are engines of progress. They are responsible for the vast majority of the forward progress and positive change we see in the world. Projects remain the best mechanism we have to turn our visions, goals, and hopes for the future into reality. And the men and women who lead them are the unsung superheroes of our time.

But delivering successful projects has become much tougher in the volatile, uncertain, complex, and ambiguous (VUCA) environment in which we live. The problems we need to solve are more complex, the risks are higher, and the pressure on us to deliver solutions intensifies.

These factors impose new demands on the already tough job leaders face in guiding their organizations and project teams.

But on the plus side, the opportunities to deliver innovative projects that make a real difference are far greater as well.

These dynamics make it incumbent for all project leaders and teams to continually update their strategic skills and learn better approaches in order to handle challenges of the kind they have not faced before. That's the reason I wrote this book.

Turn Strategy into Action

Strategic Project Management Made Simple offers you a logical step-by-step approach and a common language to think more strategically, plan more effectively, and implement more smoothly in order to get better results.

The methodology in this book offers a systems thinking approach that brings together core principles from two methodologies: Strategic Planning and Project Management. While both are essential, in practice, there is often a large and costly gap between the essential strategic Goals we set and the projects intended to achieve them.

To close the gap between intended and actual results, project teams must become more strategic in their approach. That means starting with the big *Why* behind a project in order to better understand how it fits the big picture. In the same vein, senior management and others who develop strategy need to become more project-focused.

To tackle issues that are complex, we need a planning process that is simple—as simple as possible, but no simpler. Simple enough to comprehend the larger structure without being overwhelming. Simple but not simplistic. Simple enough to be easily learned and applied in any context. That is why the approach that follows is based upon four simple questions that drive the project design process, beginning with the big *Why* and then logically progress to determine the *What*, the *How*, the *Who*, and the *When*.

Project Leaders Deliver Results

My definition of a project leader is *anyone who takes responsibility for delivering results*. Whether you work for a large corporation, a small business, a government agency, a nonprofit, or you are self-employed, by stepping up and assuming responsibility, you are indeed a project leader.

Your job title may not include the words *Project Leader*, but the fact that you are reading this book defines you as one. By investing your time here, you distinguish yourself as someone committed to making the biggest positive impact you can as well as to be of service to others.

Preparing for the Changing World Ahead

The interrelated crises of 2020 remind us how suddenly the world can dramatically change. In addition to the tragic loss of so many lives, COVID-19 sparked an economic and business crisis that disrupted virtually every aspect of how we lived, worked, played, and socialized.

The after-effects of these shock waves will continue to ripple throughout this decade and beyond, requiring innovative responses within every type of organization.

Multiple other change factors are always in play, among them changing customer expectations, advancing technology, demographic shifts, global competitors, and political factors, not to mention climate change and the global economy.

So, buckle up and prepare yourself to navigate through a fast-paced, complex, and constantly changing environment. Be prepared to face problems and seize opportunities of the type never before experienced. When you are equipped with the right tools—even if the ride gets bumpy at times—you can weather the turbulence and reach your destination.

What Project Teams Require

Project teams come in all types, sizes, shapes, and forms. The most innovative and future-oriented work will be accomplished by project teams in a variety of configurations, including cross-functional task forces, intact work units, distributed virtual teams, and ad hoc groups across a broad business landscape.

Because technology makes it possible for team members to be located anywhere on the planet, projects often bring together new casts of characters who are diverse in many dimensions. Diverse technically. Diverse culturally. Diverse in ethnicity, geography, native language, personality. Diverse in their values, thinking style and working approach. Diversity can be a strength, but it also makes it difficult to get started when team members lack a common planning approach.

When new project teams come together, they need to organize, develop a sound plan, and move into action. To do so, they need a simple step-by-step approach, a shared project vocabulary, and a logical organizing structure for their plan. The Logical Framework Approach featured in this book meets that requirement.

Who This Book Is For

Over the years, I have applied, evolved, and fine-tuned this approach in high-tech, low-tech, and no-tech organizations in business, government, and nonprofits all across the globe. The concepts that follow are universally applicable and will benefit anyone who is committed to making a positive impact. How you apply them depends on your role.

Senior managers—including CEOs, executive sponsors, program managers, strategic planners, and department heads—will find a logical language to clearly communicate and share strategic intent with those who execute critical projects.

Project teams, task forces, and change agents will discover a more rapid and thorough way to get projects going faster as they simultaneously build a strong team and an effective plan.

If you are an entrepreneur, consultant, or wild-eyed visionary, these ideas will help you focus on what is most important to you in achieving your mission.

This book will guide you in just about everything you undertake. Whether you are starting new projects, accelerating existing ones, reinventing your business model, integrating new technology, streamlining internal operations, developing strategic plans, upgrading core processes, creating next-generation products, delivering high-quality services, serving new customers, grooming future talent, expanding your business, or pivoting your organization, just as examples, these principles apply.

What You'll Find in This Book

This book does not attempt to cover the mainstream Project Management techniques found in other books and training programs. You will not find instructions for constructing a work breakdown structure, calculating earned value, or applying other conventional project tools. Those lessons are readily available elsewhere.

What you will find here is a common-sense, systems-thinking-based approach that you can readily apply to virtually any project. This approach does not compete or conflict with the conventional project planning methodologies. In fact, it enhances them by adding a strategic perspective that is missing in most other methods. This provides an ideal front-end starting point for any project, whether you will employ agile or any other type of project lifecycle.

I wrote the first edition of this book over a decade ago to share the best strategic management practices I knew with leaders who are committed to making a positive difference in their work and lives. And I am grateful that so many people have shared with me that their project success rate has significantly increased since applying this approach. In addition, their teams experience the sense of shared accomplishment that comes from clarity of purpose and clear direction.

Combining a strong strategic skill set with a nimble mindset and a caring heart-set equips you to tackle and overcome the biggest obstacles and experience the satisfaction that comes from making a difference.

What's New in This Book

Since the first edition was published, I have coached thousands of executives, project leaders, and teams from various sectors including technology, manufacturing, research, services, gaming, government, and national security to refine their core strategies while staying true to their vision and values. In the pages ahead, I will share some of these same principles and strategies.

This totally revised and expanded second edition includes insights I have gained since the first edition, along with application innovations that readers have shared with me. You will find new sections on how to:

- Bridge the costly gap between strategic planning and project management.
- Engage and involve stakeholders throughout the project.
- Integrate this approach with agile and other emerging tools and processes.
- Create a psychologically safe environment that frees people to perform their best.
- Organize your "inner game" of thoughts and emotions to optimize your performance.
- Pivot your organization or department when conditions require a major shift.
- Apply these same principles to your personal and professional projects.

You will be guided step-by-step on how to turn your good ideas, problems, or opportunities into tangible results. In addition, you will see how other project leaders have used these same tools to engage and inspire their teams. I will also refer you to several must-read books that complement and expand on the ideas described here.

Because of all the added new material, there is no room to include several additional resources I want you to have. So, I have organized all of these valuable resources into a bonus package, which is free to anyone who bought this book. This bonus contains project design examples you can use as role models for your own similar projects. It also includes a flexible "quick and clean" Strategy Refresh Process to pivot your business or revitalize your work unit, along with other guidance to support you in implementing what you learn here. Find and download these materials at *www.ManagementPro.com /bookbonus*.

Getting the Most from Our Journey Together

This book consists of three overall parts with four chapters within each one:

- Part I explores the principles that make Strategic Project Management both simple and powerful.
- Part II builds upon that foundation, drilling down to offer step-by-step instructions about how to design executable projects.
- Part III pulls it all together and also explores the human dynamics of projects.

Throughout the chapters there are various examples and real-world case studies, along with Key Point Summaries at the end of each for quick recall.

Along the way, I share my personal story of what inspired my career path and the mentors who changed my life. My purpose in sharing my story is to encourage you to reflect on, and take pride in, your own life journey and your commitment to make a positive difference.

I encourage you to personalize this book by underlining or highlighting key sentences. Scribble your own thoughts in the margins. If you are reading on a tablet, tag what jumps out at you. And as you proceed, swirl these ideas around in your mind and try them out on your own projects in order to move the mountains in your path.

No one can foretell how the future will unfold, but one thing is for sure: We will need our collaborative thinking and coordinated action—coupled with a sense of urgency—to build the future we want in our businesses and communities. That will take all of us. You. Me. All of us. And the strategic principles of this book—when thoughtfully applied—will move aside the mountains in your path.

As you will soon discover, these principles will enable you to think bigger, plan smarter, and act faster in order to accomplish ambitious Objectives in both your professional and personal arenas. People who can do so are rare—and you are about to become one of them.

Let's get started!

Part I

Gaining the Strategic Advantage

These first four chapters examine how these Strategic Project Management concepts combine to give you a repeatable approach to creating projects with a greater likelihood of success:

- *Chapter 1* introduces core concepts and shows how they benefit your projects, your teams, your organization, and your career.
- *Chapter 2* explores a fundamental principle that serves as the backbone of any strategy or project and is at the heart of this common-sense approach.
- *Chapter 3* covers the art of setting project objectives that clearly align with the broader strategy.
- *Chapter 4* explains the solution tool and invites you to see how it transformed a poorly performing organization.

1

Developing Your Strategic
Project Mindset

*We cannot solve problems with the same thinking we used when
we created them.*

—Albert Einstein

This chapter launches you on the path to understanding fresh ways
to design and deliver projects that produce measurable benefits.

The systems thinking approach to projects that follows has been
proven across a wide variety of industries and project types. Applying
this process reduces the gap between strategic goals and the project
action plans needed to reach those goals.

This chapter offers a preview of the Logical Framework, a solution approach that gives you a competitive advantage in both your
professional work and personal life, even in uncertain times. This
organizing tool and four critical strategic questions will help you to
design effective project strategies that propel your organization and
career forward.

And it shares a timeless lesson NASA learned the hard way,
along with my personal story.

What NASA Rule #15 Can Teach Us

Early in my career I was fortunate to work with the National Aeronautics and Space Administration (NASA), where I developed an obsession with designing and delivering ambitious projects. But you do not have to be a rocket scientist to appreciate NASA Rule #15, which states:

> The seeds of problems are laid down early. Initial planning is the most vital part of a project. The review of most failed projects and project problems indicated that the disasters were well-planned to happen from the start.
> —NASA Rule #15

Can you relate? Have you experienced project problems that could have been avoided with more effective initial planning? If so, you are not alone.

Based on my experience observing how project teams typically plan their projects, I see three ways that "problem seeds" get planted early:

First, by using planning approaches and tools that are overly complex, restrictive, or ill-suited to producing the type of actionable plans that are needed. The mandated approach in some organizations is so inadequate that people often resort to just filling out the required forms without first truly understanding the project context and strategic objectives.

Second, failing to recognize the multiple other factors that are necessary for project success but that are not part of the project. Every project is a puzzle piece in a larger picture, and not understanding the strategic connections during project design can result in ignoring the risks that can doom any project.

The third mistake teams frequently make is to prematurely focus on *How* the project will be done before thoroughly and thoughtfully understanding *Why* the project should be done. Such project plans, even when well implemented, seldom achieve the expected impact.

My commitment is to guide you through a simple, logical, and flexible planning approach that can overcome these problems and move your project team into motion more quickly and easily. In my experience, this approach can cut upfront project planning time by two-thirds while doubling your chances for success.

Close the Strategy-to-Execution Gap

In recent years, the Project Management Institute, the International Project Management Association, the Association for Strategic Planning, and other professional associations have broadened their scope to emphasize the linkages between strategy and projects. These are huge gaps between these two critical functions that result in a staggering waste of human and financial resources that we can ill afford.

According to *Fortune*, 70 percent of all strategies fail because they could not be implemented, even though the strategies themselves were sound. *Forbes* estimates 54 percent of technology project failures can be attributed to poor management, while only 3 percent were due to technology issues. It should be clear that using simple concepts that enable people to think through and logically connect projects with strategic goals is part of the solution.

The Power of Systems Thinking

A few years ago, I was recruited by the president of the Association for Strategic Planning (ASP) to help develop a rigorous program to certify strategic planners. Back then, anyone whose business card said "strategic planner" could claim to be one. There were no common standards, skill requirements, or means to certify those who were competent.

One of my assignments involved working with Howard Rohm, the president of the Balanced Scorecard Institute. We evaluated the common elements behind the most effective strategic planning approaches, and the number one criterion we identified was all the effective approaches were based upon *systems-thinking principles*.

Systems thinking takes a wide-angle holistic view that situates projects in the larger context in which they operate. It considers how things influence each other—that is, how a project affects and is affected by the organization, system, or context in which it operates.

Systems thinking is also called strategic thinking, big picture thinking, discovery thinking, critical thinking, solutions thinking, ideation, long-term thinking, and high-level thinking. Systems thinking is in contrast to the widespread use of *analytic* or *linear* thinking, which is piecemeal and narrow in scope. Analytic thinking comes into play when we are mapping out the details of a project, but we need to start with systems thinking that can produce the desired impact. Following this personal background story, we'll introduce a systems thinking approach to projects.

Shoot for the Moon

Let me share a bit about my life's journey, so you understand how these ideas developed. I will begin the story here and add additional parts later.

My dad was a bulldozer operator working on construction projects in the Pacific Northwest. Our family of four (plus a dog, as well as a bowl of small but intrepid guppies) lived in a 244-square-foot trailer house. When one construction project would end, we just hitched up the trailer to the pickup truck and moved to the next one.

Because we would usually move in the middle of the school year, I went to eight different elementary schools in four different states before high school. You could say my life was "agile." Arriving mid-school year forced me to quickly figure out which kids to hang around with and which ones to avoid, what the teachers were like, and what I could get away with and not. Today, I would call that "stakeholder analysis."

How My Rocket Career Started

I remember a day that shaped my life direction. I was sitting in my fifth-grade math class in Weaverville, California, on October 4, 1957, when my teacher, Mrs. Smith, rushed in to announce the Soviet Union had launched a satellite into earth's orbit! That night, my family huddled around a 17-inch, black-and-white television in our cramped living room to watch a fuzzy broadcast of CBS news anchor Walter Cronkite announce that *Sputnik 1* had begun a new era—The Space Age.

Mr. Cronkite would soon have a much greater impact on my life and career than just watching him on the *CBS Evening News*. But I am getting ahead of myself. That part of my story will have to wait until Chapter 5.

While I did not understand the geopolitical implications, I knew rockets and satellites were way cooler than my electric trains. So, I started building rockets with the resources at hand. I built my first rocket by wrapping aluminum foil around the end of a pencil to create a hollow cylinder, and then removed the pencil and filled the cylinder with match heads. I would twist the aluminum foil into a nozzle of sorts; then light it up and stand back. They would go *pfffftt* and fly about two feet. A promising start to my rocket career!

A Bold Presidential Declaration

The next major milestone that influenced my career direction occurred in high school, when President John F. Kennedy committed the United States to landing a man on the moon with his famous declaration to Congress.

> I believe that this Nation should commit itself to achieving the goal, before this decade is out, of landing a man on the Moon and returning him safely to Earth.
> —John F. Kennedy, May 25, 1961

The man Kennedy put in charge of this ambitious mission was Dr. Wernher von Braun, director of the NASA Marshall Space Flight Center in Huntsville, Alabama. That is where America would build the massive *Saturn V* moon rocket. Von Braun was a German rocket scientist who was brought to the United States with the rest of his team at the end of World War II. (See Figure 1.1.)

Oh, how I longed to be a "Rocket Man" just like him! He was brilliant, handsome, bold, and visionary—everything this nerdy kid was not but yearned to be. My dream was to meet him in person one day.

Four years later would find me writing letters to von Braun—and with no idea of the impact they were about to have on my life . . . oops! Getting ahead of myself again. We will have to come back to that story episode a little later.

Send Living Creatures into Inner Space

My next rocket project came when I was a high school sophomore. It was a true experiment, although there was something fishy about it. I figured *If* I launched something alive, *Then* I could become a "Rocket

FIGURE 1.1 My First Heroic Role Model

Man" myself. And *If* I became a Rocket Man, *Then* I could help put people on the moon.

While I did not know it at the time, by working backwards from the big *Why* goal of putting people on the moon, I was doing strategic thinking in my mind. We can do this all more or less intuitively, but we usually miss key steps and do not leverage the potential of this basic logic when designing our projects.

At that time, amateur "rocketeers" like myself were making model rockets with pre-built engines made by the Estes company to launch crickets and cockroaches into the air. Boring passengers! It had been done before. I needed to make a bigger splash by launching more impressive living creatures to build my Rocket Man credentials.

But what? Finding living creatures small enough was a challenge. Mice? Too heavy. Frogs? Too bulky. Then I eyed my sister

Cheryl's two (soon-to-be intrepid) guppies, Minnie and Mickey, who lived in a glass jar on the kitchen counter. They were the perfect size and weight. After I bribed her with chocolate, she reluctantly agreed to let me borrow them.

HALO 1 was a one-foot-tall model rocket topped with a water-tight plastic passenger capsule, ¾ inch in diameter. This would house the two volunteer fish who had no idea of their coming adventure. Attached to the passenger capsule was a plastic parachute designed to allow the precious payload to descend gently.

I wish you could have been with us on that bright, sunny Saturday on the 50-yard line of the football field in Paradise High School in California. Watching from the sidelines were my proud parents, hopeful buddies, and one very anxious sister, Cheryl.

I assembled *HALO 1* on its launch pad, filled the capsule with water, carefully loaded the unaware guppies, sealed the nose cone with Scotch tape, and began the countdown.

10-9-8-7-6. . . (Action: Light the fuse)

5-4-3-2-1 (Action: Stand back)

Lift off!

HALO 1 shot up like a *rocket*, leaving a trail of smoke. It should have reached 2,000 feet, but halfway up it broke apart, the parachute failed, and the passenger capsule came plummeting down towards the goalposts. I rushed to the end zone with my portable water-filled recovery van (which was actually a Chinese food takeout container). Fortunately, the capsule fell onto soft grass, unbroken.

But half of the water was gone from the capsule and my intrepid volunteers were twisted into shapes few tiny fish ever experience. My scientific conclusion was that guppies are not designed for the unexpected 3-G force of takeoff (at least not without training).

I ripped off the Scotch tape that sealed the passenger capsule and dumped the fish into the recovery van. When they sank to the bottom, my heart sank with them. Oh no! There goes my rocket career.

But a subtle fin flicker suggested they were not dead, but were merely unconscious. I discovered that by gently blowing on them, dipping them into water, blowing and dipping, blowing and dipping back and forth, they began to wiggle and slowly regained consciousness.

I wrote a story about the experience for *Model Rocket News* that gained wide attention and convinced me to pursue an aerospace engineering degree at the University of Washington, as part of the plan to further my budding rocket career. (See Figure 1.2.)

MODEL ROCKET NEWS

Guppies Into Inner Space
—or—
There's Something Fishy There

by Terry Schmidt

It looked like a good day. The clouds had cleared and the sky was inviting. Two guppies about 3/4" long had been obtained two days before, and they appeared strong and ready for the trip. It was Saturday, February 2, and the early morning hours were spent in last minute preparations and calculations. All rocketeers arrived at launch site, and after a few delays, we were ready to launch.

The rocket was taken out to the triple launching device and assembled on pad three. The treated water, boiled to remove the impurities and poured back and forth between two containers to absorb oxygen, was poured into the capsule. The two guppies were taken from their transport van and the

FIGURE 1.2   The Dramatic Launch of *HALO 1*

Preserved for Posterity

I would like to say Minnie and Mickey escaped unharmed. Unfortunately, Minnie gained a permanent kink in her spine that caused her to spiral downward and hit bottom whenever she swam. For the rest of his life, Mickey swam level, but only in tight ¾-inch concentric circles.

They are still around, well-preserved in a small glass bottle, much like Egyptian mummies. To commemorate their historic flight and contribution to the world of rocketeering, someday I will donate these brave pioneers to the Schmidtsonian Institute for future generations to admire.

In future chapters, we will cover other episodes of my unusual Rocket Man story, and share the lessons learned along the way.

Different Contexts But Similar Issues

After earning my BS in engineering at Washington and then an MBA at Harvard, I took a job as a Program Planner in the U.S. Department of Transportation in Washington, DC, where I learned how to orchestrate strategic plans.

After three years of government work, I became an international development advisor. For several years, I trained project leaders in over 20 developing countries in Africa, Asia, Latin America, and the Middle East to design projects that improve the lives of the rural poor. That is where I mastered the power of this *systems* approach that has become the basis of my life's work with clients.

After several years of international development work, I switched my consulting practice to serve corporate, government, research, and nonprofit organizations. People in these organizations also struggled to get projects off the ground efficiently. They candidly shared their thoughts and feelings about their projects, such as:

- "We plan, but our plans fall apart when we try to execute them."
- "We have good ideas, but cannot seem to implement them."
- "The goals keep changing."
- "Teamwork is lacking and it is tough to get people moving in the same direction."
- "Nasty, unexpected surprises derail us and we spend too much time fire-fighting."
- "Opportunities evaporate because we do not move fast enough."
- "We are more than frustrated!"

The last comment came from a busy manager who was clearly angry because it took weeks to design a project that could have been done in days. Back then, I was certain my approach could help, but at the time it was geared toward the needs of development audiences.

So, I adapted it to meet business needs and began teaching it at the UCLA Extension Technical Management Program. For over three decades, thousands of project managers, mid-career professionals, and technical leaders who attended over 60 of my Strategic Project Management courses there proved the system worked by applying it to projects large and small and getting the results they sought. Some diverse examples:

- A global nonprofit health organization needing to create an enterprise management system to serve widely diverse users worldwide.
- A satellite television provider needing more sophisticated ways to combat identity theft and fraud.

- An industrial company reinventing itself after a competitor's technology breakthrough threatened their main product.
- A specialized industrial software company seeking to grow their business.
- A nuclear scientist organizing experts at national research laboratories to recover radioactive materials that could fall into the wrong hands.
- A visionary entrepreneur needing to design a Minimum Viable Product to secure substantial investor funding.
- A social service agency manager caring for mentally and physically handicapped residents needing to solve the root cause of mysterious injuries to their residents.
- A department manager in a nonprofit organization needing help to set up a Project Management Office (PMO).
- A group of video-game fanatics needing to scale their business to support the rapidly growing popularity of their new online game.
- A national research laboratory needing a long-range research strategy to integrate renewable energy into the national electrical grid.

These very different projects shared certain commonalities. None of them were simple or straightforward. They were all highly visible and the goals were important. Resources were tight, there were plenty of unknowns, and the pressure was on to deliver results. Sound similar to your projects in any way?

Coming up with the right solution was much like navigating a large maze you could walk through. Think of a time you worked your way through a maze. You knew the general direction to head toward, but not the best path to get there. That's because you were at ground level and could not easily see above the walls of the maze to understand the larger structure. As a result, you often had to backtrack through blind alleys that were dead ends, wasting time and getting frustrated. But if you could begin by elevating your perspective and get a bird's-eye view, your path to reach the end point would be much easier. So too is it with projects.

You might wonder how the same system that helped developing countries improve their education system, reduce child mortality, build an economy, grow more crops, and reduce poverty could work in very different business, technical, and cultural contexts. The reason is because the basic underlying issues and solution principles we will cover in this book are essentially the same for all situations.

Because the systems thinking concepts are universal, the potential applications of the approach are virtually limitless. Ken Howell, a Sony Electronics champion of this method, says, "Show me something this *does not* apply to."

The approach you are about to discover will give you the insights you have always sensed you needed and were missing from other approaches you have tried. Along the way, I will make things as simple as possible, but no simpler.

Preview the Solution Tools

The Logical Framework Approach (LFA), is a design methodology that facilitates project planning at a broader, more integrated, and more strategic level than traditional project planning processes. The Logical Framework Approach helps us gain a clearer understanding of how the project affects, and is affected by, factors outside the project scope. This is what we mean by systems thinking.

We will use the term *Logical Framework Approach* or *LFA* to describe the overall approach, and the term *LogFrame* or *matrix* to describe the project plans this approach produces.

Present design requires first identifying:

- Why the project is being performed,
- The impact it will have,
- How to achieve it,
- How to know it is successful,
- What the risks are, and
- What is required for success from outside the scope of the project.

When this higher-level analysis is completed, the tasks and resources needed for execution become more understandable.

This approach features four sequential steps and questions, which build on each other. Following this approach reduces the tendency to jump to task lists too early. This section offers a brief overview of the approach, which is detailed in subsequent chapters. My intention for you is when you finish this book, you will have both the knowledge and desire to apply this system to your own important projects.

How It Began

The LFA was originally developed at the management consulting firm Practical Concepts Incorporated (PCI) to help the United States Agency for International Development (USAID) plan, implement, and evaluate hundreds of projects in their global multibillion-dollar foreign aid portfolio.

At PCI, I collaborated with the LFA development team. Later I taught project teams in 24 developing countries in Asia, Latin America, and the Middle East to apply this approach. Then I shifted my business to serve corporations, nonprofits, national research laboratories, and government agencies.

A Simple Interactive Matrix Structure

We are all familiar with the five Ws (and an H) used to plan our projects: *Who, What, Why, Where, When,* and *How*. The basic Logical Framework shown in Figure 1.3 serves to visually integrate these elements into a single design canvas.

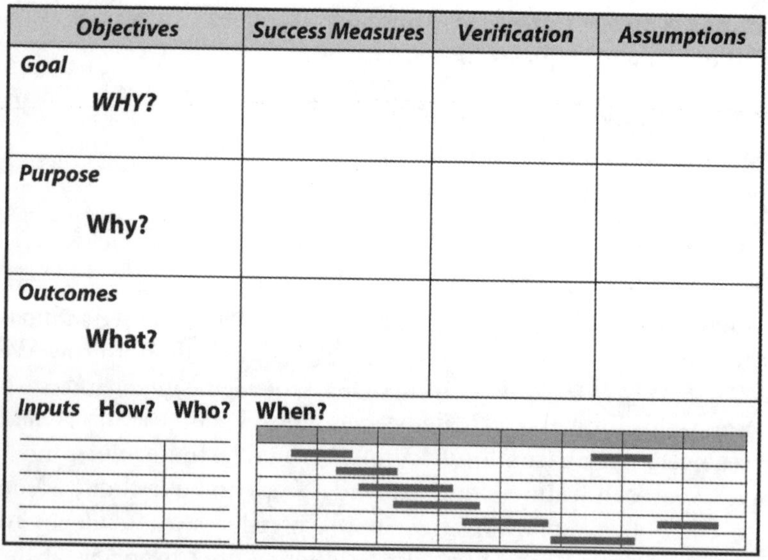

Objectives	Success Measures	Verification	Assumptions
Goal **WHY?**			
Purpose **Why?**			
Outcomes **What?**			
Inputs How? Who?	**When?**		

FIGURE 1.3 The Basic Logical Framework Matrix

This compact format can summarize and communicate a complex project in one to three pages.

The term *Logical Framework Approach* describes its essential components:

Logical	It connects various project elements together using an underlying common-sense natural language called *If-Then* construction.
Framework	It is structured as an 4×4 interactive matrix in which each cell captures project information in a specific, organized, and interlocking manner that is easily communicated.
Approach	It brings together concepts from science and management. This flexible design approach is driven by *Four Critical Strategic Questions* (below) that propel your thinking and result in an integrated plan aligned with strategic objectives.

Effective project design starts by addressing these questions, the answers to which fit into various cells in the LogFrame matrix:

1. What results are we trying to achieve, and why?
2. How do we measure success?
3. What other conditions must exist?
4. How do we get there?

The answers to Question #1 summarize the project's three main Objectives (Goal, Purpose, and Outcomes,) in the first column. Question #2 identifies the Success Measures and Verifications for each Objective in the middle two columns. Answering Question #3 fills in the Assumptions and risk factors in the last column. Question #4 summarizes the Inputs (tasks and resources), which occupy the bottom row. We will define and cover each of these elements in detail in later chapters.

By working through these questions, and organizing the results into the matrix, you create the structural foundation of your strategy. But this is not a "box-filling" exercise. The four questions guide the team dialogue and analysis, while the matrix captures the results of your thinking process in a way that is both strategic and scientific. This approach works for projects of all sizes and types.

Universal Applicators

The LogFrame has been called "the multi-bladed Swiss knife of Strategy" because it performs so many useful functions, serving as a:

- Project design canvas
- Project justification tool
- Solutions discovery tool
- Experiment design tool
- Strategy clarification tool
- Communications tool
- Alignment tool
- Team building tool
- Responsibility clarification tool
- Baseline reference tool
- Impact evaluation tool
- Process improvement tool

What triggers the need for a LogFrame? Virtually any problem, opportunity, event, or situation including these:

- New project starting with knowing little more than the end Goal.
- A list of Goals taken from a strategic plan or SWOT analysis.
- Finding a nasty surprise making you pivot your plan.
- That tough problem that needs a well-thought-out solution.
- Teams needing sharper focus and better coordination.
- Determining the feasibility of an idea.
- Business processes gone awry and needing to be reined in.
- Discovering an opportunity to exploit before the window closes.
- Encountering change that demands a response.
- Uncovering a promising idea.
- Plugging a performance gap.
- Testing a wild hunch that needs testing.

The power of the LogFrame is not in its matrix format per se, but in how its structure and embedded internal logic force team members to think through all of the critical issues as they develop solutions.

Notes on Terminology and Formatting

There are seven terms that have a specific meaning when used in the context of a LogFrame, and these are capitalized for clarity: Goal, Objectives, Purpose, Outcomes, Inputs, Success Measures (or

Measures), and Assumptions. When used in a general sense, these terms are not capitalized. In addition, the terms Why, What, Where, When, Who, and How are also capitalized and italicized when they refer to specific sections in the Logical Framework matrix. The word Vision is always capitalized.

The heart of designing projects with the LogFrame approach involves identifying causal relationships between various project Objectives. The words *If* and *Then* are capitalized and in italics to highlight when such relationships.

I'll use the terms *project strategy* and *project design* somewhat interchangeably in what follows, as well as *projects* and *strategic initiatives*.

People ask whether the book title *Strategic Project Management* refers to the management of the most *strategic* projects and special initiatives, or whether it means taking a strategic approach *to any* project. The answer is that it is both. Certainly the most critical projects demand a strategic approach, but even the simplest projects exist within a larger context and can benefit by viewing them through a strategic lens as well.

Universal Applications

This methodology is neither complicated nor abstract. Although it is simple and straightforward, applying it does take effort. But once you get the hang of it, you will save and reduce headaches.

That completes the brief Logical Framework Approach overview. We will discuss this in greater depth when we get to Chapter 4. Then, in Chapters 5–8, we take a deep dive into each of the four questions, so you have a complete understanding of a flexible power tool that belongs in the toolbox of every knowledge worker and project leader.

But before we do that, let us first set the groundwork in Chapter 2 and Chapter 3 by exploring the LogFrame's most essential underlying principles—those of logic and those of language. My intent is to show you how this system works, but more importantly, for you to understand *why* it works.

Review Key Points

1. Strategic Project Management provides more flexible ways to think, plan, and act, and is a must-have skill for everyone in these uncertain times.

2. Initial planning is the most critical part of any project (NASA's Rule #15). Clearly identify *Why* the project is needed before deciding *How* it will be done.

3. The three vital factors for smooth initial planning are a common language, a common process, and an organized framework.

4. The LogFrame gives you a competitive edge to succeed in almost every type of project by reducing the gap between strategy development and execution.

5. Your ability to turn an idea into a well-designed and actionable project provides you with a potent competitive advantage. And this book gives you the keys to gain that advantage.

Coming Up Next

The need for committed and capable project leaders like you who can think strategically and turn ideas into action has never been higher. In the next chapter, we will introduce a design principle missing from most other project design methods. We are going to build a project strategy using cause-and-effect logic chains by "starting with the end in mind," and working backwards to identify each step required to ensure the project can achieve the impact intended.

2

Visualizing Project Strategy

Shallow people believe in luck or in circumstance. Strong people believe in cause and effect.

—Ralph Waldo Emerson

Imagine you have been given the job of creating and communicating the strategy for an important project in your organization. How are you going to approach it?

In this chapter, we will introduce two simple visual tools to assist you. These two tools are *Causality* and *Objectives Trees*, and they add value in every strategic management scenario.

We first explore *causality*, also called *cause and effect*, or *If-Then* thinking. Causality is the "special sauce" that differentiates this approach from most others.

Then we move on to *Objectives Trees*. Objectives Trees are a way to visually display and work out the underlying logic chains relevant to your project. To master this design tool enables you to design projects from a strategic perspective.

Following these precepts will give you the capacity to communicate the big *Why* of your project and the benefits it will deliver.

Let us begin by exploring how to align Goals and Projects with Vision and Strategy.

Make Simple Strategy

I have taught Strategic Management for dozens of years all across the globe. From this experience it has become clear to me even though many books talk about Mission, Vision, Strategy, Goals, Projects, and Objectives, they do not offer simple ways to bring these concepts together to craft executable projects from a strategic perspective.

The following discussion and my project design approach itself follows the KISS Principle: *Keep It Simple, Schmidt*. In fact, the strength of this system is its ability to capture the complexity of a project in clear and straightforward ways.

A simple definition of strategy is knowing where you want to be in the future (Vision); how you plan to get there (Goals and Projects); and the stream of decisions you make along the way (Agile execution).

Begin with Vision

Every organization, from a Fortune 500 company to a small business, to a family, to even oneself, has some sense of what its *Vision* is. A Vision statement expresses why the entity exists, and the guiding principles it believes necessary to accomplishing its work. We can think of a Vision as the ultimate "North Star" Objective that offers the ultimate inspiration and clarification regarding how to invest resources.

Goals are what moves the organization towards its Vision. Goals are statements of future intent that require one or more projects to achieve them, as shown in Figure 2.1 For example, a company with a Vision to be a leading supplier of a product must, among other things, achieve Goals such as a solid profit margin and wide customer acceptance. Each of those Goals requires contributions from projects and operations across several disciplines.

Projects are the organized and focused efforts that contribute to reaching any Goal. This is where the LogFrame comes in, to help you establish a strong linkage between your Project and its intended impact on the Goal.

Notice the simple logical relationships built into Figure 2.1. Starting up from the bottom of the diagram and looking upwards, we can presume that:

- *If* we do projects well, *Then* we achieve certain Goals.
- *If* we achieve these Goals, *Then* we contribute to the Vision.

From Objectives Tree to Project Portfolio

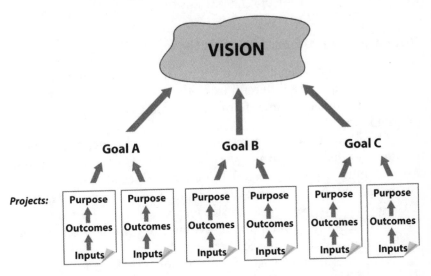

FIGURE 2.1   Projects Achieve Goals That Support a Vision

One benefit of this simple *If-Then* connectivity is that you can construct logical paths from project tasks all the way up to the Vision.

This cause-effect, *If-Then* logic constitutes a *hypothesis*, an "educated guess" about what it will take to reach a goal. Having mentioned how *If-Then* logic can define and clarify strategies all the way up to Vision, let's examine more deeply the principle that binds it all together.

The Power of Causal Logic

Throw a ball into the air and the force of gravity acting on it eventually brings it back down to the earth. The upward force of throwing was the *cause* that produced the *effect* of the ball rising, as the downward force of gravity was the *cause* that produced the *effect* of the ball returning to the ground. Expressed using *If-Then* terms . . .

- *If* you throw a ball vertically, *Then* it will rise.
- *If* the ball rises, *Then* the force of gravity will bring it down to the ground.

Every Goal is reached because of a carefully thought-out chain of logical cause-and-effect relationships that lead up to it.

Distinguish Causal from Sequential Logic

The *causal* logic which links the four levels of Objectives in the LogFrame matrix is different from the *sequential* logic commonly used in network diagrams, flowcharts, Gannt charts, and computer programming.

Here's the critical distinction: In sequential logic, A precedes B in time and defines a pathway towards it. It describes the condition where A must happen before B. Note that A does not *cause* B; it simply *precedes* it. However, with causal logic, A not only precedes B, but A causes B to happen (or at least contributes to it). This may seem like a distinction without a difference, but it is central to understanding how to think about projects strategically.

With causal logic, it is not enough for one event to occur *prior to* a second, the first must be *required by* and *contribute to* the second. The rooster crows before dawn, but his crowing does not cause the sun to rise.

The essence of strategy—how to get to where you want to be—is embedded directly in the language of causal linkages. When you design your project around well-thought-out causal sequences, you increase the probability of achieving the intended impact. If you cannot sketch out the linkages, you may not have a promising strategy. It's hard to achieve what you cannot describe.

As this book unfolds, you will appreciate how applying this simple principle helps to build a strong structural foundation for your project from the very beginning.

Put on Your Scientist Hat

Maybe you saw the movie *Field of Dreams*, where Kevin Costner's character contemplates building a baseball field in the middle of an Iowa cornfield. One night while in the cornfield, he hears a mysterious voice, "*If* you build it, [*Then*] they will come." That was his simple two-level hypothesis—and it carried a good deal of uncertainty.

Approach your project the way a scientist would, as a carefully structured experiment. You design your project experiment by identifying a presumed set of hypotheses that you believe will work but that you need to test. That is, you believe "A" will produce Objective "B," and "B" will in turn produce Objective "C," and so on. Your belief comes from your life experience, knowledge, data, and best judgment. The results you get during implementation will determine the validity of your hypotheses.

You do not have to be a scientist to design projects in a way that is strategic, scientific, and street-smart. You may not win the Nobel Prize, but the quality of your results will be worthy of gold medals. Now let's explore causal logic further, and show how you can apply it to your own endeavors.

Construct Simple Logic Chains

Figure 2.2 offers examples of single chains of Objectives, linked according to our *If-Then* principle. The upward arrows show the logical relationships going vertically upwards from the bottom. You can also read it from the top down to see dependencies; each Objective is dependent on the one below it. We refer to this as *bidirectional thinking*.

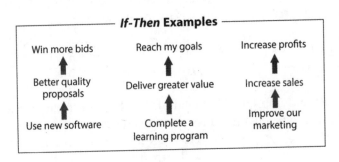

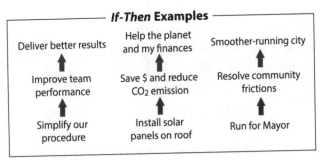

FIGURE 2.2 **Single Chains of Objectives**

The higher-level Objectives in the hierarchy tend to be broader, more general, influenced by other factors than just your present project. The lower-level Objectives tend to be more specific and concrete.

Design Top-Down, Deliver Bottom-Up

We generally design our projects with some sense of the Goal, then work down to determine the lower-level Objectives, all the way down to tasks. When done, we can mentally test the soundness of the implementation plan by working bottom up, asking, "Will this Objective contribute to achieving the next-highest Objective?" If our logic does not hold up, we must rethink it.

Consider the example in the top upper right corner of Figure 2.2. Starting with the Objective to increase profits, ask, "What is necessary to reach this Objective?" One way to do that is to increase sales. And in turn, that can happen if we improve our marketing.

This is important: Any project hypothesis can be summarized by a set of logical *If-Then* linkages. We generate the project design using causal logic from the top down, starting with the Objective at the top, and work backwards (down) to identify what is needed to make that happen. We can then check this logic by reading from the bottom up, where the sequence is expressed as:

- *If* we improve our marketing, *Then* we will increase sales.
- *If* we increase sales, *Then* we will increase profits.

When reading our logic chain from the bottom up, notice there are a few things missing. First, increasing sales to increase profits only works *assuming* other factors do not change, such as overhead costs. In a later chapter we will expand our logic chain to include Assumptions, but for now will keep it very basic.

We also notice increasing marketing to increase sales is not the only way to increase profits. What about reducing overhead or improving efficiency? This is where Objectives Trees come in.

Organize Objectives into Trees

Objectives Trees display potential alternate paths to reach any Goal. They expand a single chain of linked Objectives into branches, which show multiple options that can be considered and compared.

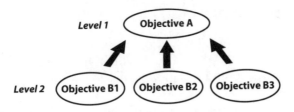

FIGURE 2.3   Generic Objectives Tree Structure

The easiest way to visualize an Objectives Tree is to use an inverted tree diagram as shown in Figure 2.3. In this example we are looking for ways to achieve Objective A by considering and comparing three potential supporting Objectives B1, B2, and B3.

We can "trim the tree" by eliminating the less desirable branches and leave only those (one or more) we will pursue. In the Figure 2.3 example, we may determine after analysis that Level 2 Objectives B1 and B3 are both required to achieve the Level 1 Objective A, but Objective B2 is not. We would then flesh out Log-Frame project plans for Objectives B1 and B3. We can more precisely analyze which branches yield the most fruit by adding Success Measures, a topic we will explore in Chapter 6.

There are several things to note about Objectives Trees:

1. They clarify the possible alternatives as you shape your strategy and help you choose the best path.
2. The Objectives Tree can extend down multiple levels in order to analyze and select the mix of best strategy elements.
3. By adding Success Measures for each Objective, we can better evaluate options.
4. Objectives Trees are helpful, but they are incomplete and imperfect statements of causal relationships. They become more valid by identifying the Assumptions needed to make the logic valid.

Illuminate Multiple Solution Paths

There are various ways you can use Objectives Trees to illuminate solution paths. Consider the following examples.

Example: Improve Profits

Consider the example Objectives Tree in Figure 2.4. The top-level Objective is to improve profits. Reading from the top down, you can identify two potential logical paths for *how* you might achieve that Purpose.

In most cases, rather than an either-or choice, the best strategies are a combination of several choices. There are many ways to draw these trees, and several variations are shown in this book.

These simple diagrams provide a starting point for deeper analysis. The visual imagery triggers creative thinking and helps you to identify your best approaches. For bigger issues, you may even find your tree contains several potential projects, some of which you may want to split out, as shown in Figure 2.5. Your analysis of strategic contribution, resources, feasibility, and priorities will influence which projects move forward now, and which would be considered later.

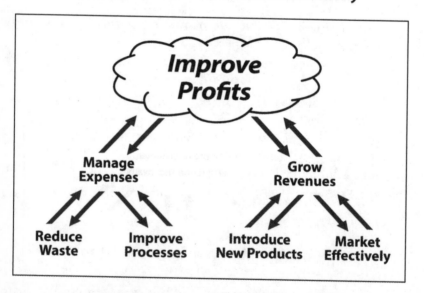

FIGURE 2.4   Improve Profits Objectives Tree

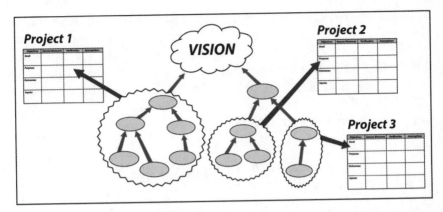

FIGURE 2.5 Objectives Trees Identify Project Possibilities

Example: Solve the Customer Support Problem

Company X was a small but fast-growing software company that served an important need in a niche market. Their product was good but complicated. As a result, many users needed help and called the understaffed Customer Support department. The staff were overwhelmed, and customers were frustrated by the long wait times and the need to call back multiple times.

The Customer Support team strategized about how to fix the problem and sketched out some possible ways to improve customer satisfaction and loyalty. They considered three different approaches as shown in the bottom row of Figure 2.6.

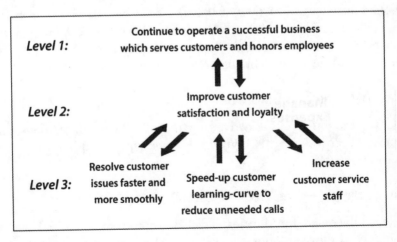

FIGURE 2.6 Improve Customer Satisfaction Alternative Tree

Because resources were limited, they could not do all three. Thus, they evaluated each option according to three criteria—cost to implement, time required, and probable impact on customer satisfaction. From these criteria, they were able to quickly exclude the option to increase staff and chose to implement both of the remaining options.

We will return to this example in Chapter 6 and build out a project plan from this starting point.

Develop Your Own Objectives Tree

You do not always need an Objectives Tree. If your project is reasonably simple, clear, and stands alone, you can skip this step and go straight to a LogFrame. But if your project is large, complex, or embedded in a larger context, sketching out an Objectives Tree will give better visibility to alternative approaches for developing the strategy.

This creative design process is facilitated by using sticky-notes. By writing the possible tasks and objectives on sticky-notes, you can then paste them to a whiteboard, move things around, see how one idea leads to another, and draw connecting lines. Voilà, a strategy map! Remote teams can do this with the right online collaboration tools.

Generate an Initial List of Objectives

Brainstorm as many potential Objectives as possible without attempting to analyze or structure them. (In Chapter 3, we will explore more about Objectives.) For now, make sure each begins with a verb followed by a one-to four-word description. If you have written documents, use them to get started. You can also begin with a mind map to get lots of ideas on the table before creating your Objectives Tree.

Identify the Highest Objective

Identify the top-level Objective to which all others will relate. Sometimes you are given this high-level statement, but other times you must derive it.

Extend the Objectives Tree One Level Down

Select Objectives for the next level down from your initial list, or generate additional ones by asking, "How might we accomplish the upper-level Objectives?" Draw lines to connect the lower-level Objectives to those they support.

As you work your whiteboard, you might wonder if a given Objective is useful or not. You can ask if it is actually required. That is when you review the next level up with the question, "Why is this task/step/resource required in this project?" Looking at the level above should answer this question.

Continue to Extend the Tree to the Next Lowest Level

Continue working down from the top by asking the questions "How can this Objective be accomplished?" "What lower-level or contributing Objectives are necessary to reach the higher Objective?" Continue this process until you get to the level where you might start detailing actual tasks and resources.

Review and Refine the Logic

You may discover some Objectives are vague or appear incomplete. If so, clarify or restate them. If the "jump" between levels seems too large, add intermediate Objectives. Not everything on your brainstorm list will logically fit. Do not force it. As you review, other Objectives will emerge that are not obvious until you make the effort to really *think* about the linkages.

Test the Logic

When you have your tree more or less completed, it is time to test the logic by verifying the causal relationships you have identified between the levels, using the *If-Then* construct.

Sketching out Objectives Trees is not a trivial or superfluous exercise. As basic as they seem, they force you to think about the problem and its possible solutions from multiple angles. Considering your project from this strategic perspective enables you to identify alternative approaches as well as spot flaws or gaps in your strategy.

The real contribution of visual tools like this is to guide conversations and clarify options. They do not have to be perfect to be useful.

I have witnessed project teams sketching out Objectives Trees together become energized and enthused as they discover new pathways to reach their solution.

    I encourage CEOs, department heads, and project planners to use Objectives Trees when initiating high-level or complex strategies and projects. Doing so will demonstrate to others how it fits in the larger scheme of things. Better yet, do so collaboratively with the project leader and team. This will trigger a robust and informative discussion, which aligns the project with strategic intent.

Review Key Points

1. The unique perspective of the Logical Framework Approach is that every project is based upon chains of *If-Then* causal links.
2. Each causal link is an uncertain hypothesis (or educated guess). A well-designed causal sequence reduces risk and increases the probability your project will have an impact on the Goal.
3. Appreciate the difference between causal sequences and not just sequential ones. In both, X precedes Y, but only in causal logic does X cause or contribute to Y. Causal logic is what integrates the four Objectives levels.
4. Learn to think bidirectionally. Start at the top with your biggest *Why* Objective and work down, at each step answering *How* you will achieve the Objective above it. When done, design logic in order to determine the following: Why you are implementing each Objective, and how the project will be executed.
5. *Design* projects from the top down beginning with a Goal, but *deliver* them from the bottom up beginning with the project Inputs (tasks and resources).
6. The ability to be a bidirectional thinker is a Strategic Superpower that belongs in every Project Leader's toolkit.
7. Before solidifying your project strategy, construct an Objectives Tree to help compare alternatives and identify the optimum approach.

Coming Up Next

Imagine that you are presenting to your senior leaders the strategy for your next project, and you notice not only their eyes slowly glazing over but one or two leaders leaning back in their chairs to peek at their cell phones. That is the moment you realize there is a communication barrier you did not anticipate.

To communicate new concepts there must be a common language and common terms that are clear to everyone engaged in the project. The next chapter provides you with that common language and the terms you can use to explain the project and the strategy to others. You will learn how all types of results and intentions can be grouped into only four levels or types, and how these four form the strategy backbone of any project.

3

Speaking a Common Language

And the nicest thing about not planning is that failure comes as a complete surprise rather than being preceded by a period of worry and depression.

—Anonymous

Collaborative project design involves developing a shared Vision of the future state with a clear plan to get there. While this may seem elementary, many project teams that thought they were all aligned towards common goals find out later, when breakdowns occur, it was not the case. In this chapter, we will provide language structures and templates to create that shared Vision by constructing strategy maps.

This chapter introduces a simple vocabulary grounded in meaningful design principles.

We will look at how the popular practice of "SMART" Goals and Objectives can be improved. We also introduce a master list of verbs to get your project design humming. Then we discuss the concept of "chunking" to artfully divide a project into manageable parts. You will see how every project can be designed using just four levels or types of linked Objectives.

Communicate with Clarity

If you have ever been to a country where you did not speak the local language, and they did not speak yours, you know the problem. Repeating yourself did not help. You spoke louder and they still did not understand. Despite a mutual desire to communicate, you just could not. As a result, you may have ended up with the wrong directions, hotel room, or . . . worse!

Project teams, especially newly formed and cross-functional ones, face a similar challenge. Effective communication requires a shared vocabulary, so people from dissimilar technical and cultural backgrounds can understand each other and work together. That shared vocabulary should be based on meaningful management concepts and clear definitions.

Add Language Clarity to SMART Goals

You have heard of SMART Goals and Objectives, and you may even use them. The letters stand for **S**pecific, **M**easurable, **A**chievable, **R**elevant, and **T**ime-bound. SMART Goals have been around since George Doran introduced them in a 1981 issue of *Management Review*.

The LogFrame adds additional clarifications to the SMART framework:

- All possible Objectives can be organized into just four types or levels
- Each type of Objective performs a different function in a project
- There is a logical if-then relationship among the four types of Objectives (as discussed in Chapter 2)
- The terms Goal and Objectives are related but different

Many people use the terms "Goals" and "Objectives" interchangeably, but that is like saying "French Poodles" and "Dogs" express the same thing. Let me explain.

Who Let the Dogs Out?

Are you a dog lover too? Your furry pal may be a Shih Tzu, a German Shepherd, a dog from one of the 340 other breeds recognized by the

World Canine Organization, or maybe just a lovable mutt. Regardless, it is still a dog, a *category* of creatures. Each breed is a specific *type* within that category.

Similarly, words used in management like Vision, Results, Purpose, Intent, Outcome, Output, Deliverable, Tasks, Activities, Objectives, and Goal are a single category of similar concepts, with little distinction often made between them. Just as a Golden Retriever is one type of dog, a Goal is simply one type of *Objective*. We define Objectives as *desired results of the project*.

In the LogFrame, we focus on four levels of Objectives, which we label as follows: Goal, Purpose, Outcomes, and Input. Other people might use different labels, but what's important is the concept behind the label.

Set Clear Objectives

The legendary football coach Vince Lombardi would start each season's training camp with the basics by saying to his highly skilled and highly paid players, "Gentlemen, this is a football." So, let us also start with the basics, beginning with what constitutes an objective. Each of these statements below constitutes a properly stated Objective (or desired results). Can you identify what is common in each statement?

- Reduce production cycle time
- Increase network security
- Revamp our inventory system
- Fix sub-assembly X
- Conduct a focus group
- Decrease employee turnover

- Generate more revenues
- Improve service delivery
- Upgrade our systems
- Deliver customer value
- Streamline our process
- Sell more products
- Increase brand awareness
- Organize the department

The Formula for Clear Objectives

The common feature in each of the above objectives begins with a well-chosen action verb followed by an object (also called a *descriptive*).

If you wish, you can start with the word "to" before each Objective.

Here is the simple formula for writing a clear Objective. Construct a sentence or descriptive phrase using a carefully selected *action verb* and an *object*. The object describes what is changed or acted upon, while the verb describes the action to effect the change.

Clear Objectives = Action Verb + **Object**

While each objective listed above is straightforward, they do not indicate how each relates to other objectives in the project. But we can expand these single objectives into meaningful chains of multiple objectives by using certain *connector* words, such as the following:

- To
- Thus
- Through

- By
- So that
- Because

- In order to
- That will
- Then

Note how the connector words in *italics* below can be used to logically connect single objectives into a multilevel hypothesis.

- Reduce production cycle time *in order to* launch products faster *so that* we increase market share.
- Conduct a focus group for a product idea *that will* provide necessary information, *thus* letting us decide whether to produce the product.
- Relocate 130 giraffes within four African countries *so that* we help reclaim six million acres of giraffe habitat, *thus* contributing to saving giraffes in the wild.
- Simplify internal procedures *so that* staff can understand them better *in order to* operate more efficiently.
- Have the critical parts we purchase be tested by an independent lab *so that* we reduce the risk of expensive equipment failing prematurely, *thus* protecting the value of our assets.

Three Ways to Communicate Your Project Design

You now have three ways to develop and communicate the logic behind your project design. First, you can use connector words.

We want to reduce project cycle time *in order to* launch products faster and *thus* increase market share.

Second, you can apply the *If-Then* construct.

- *If* we reduce production cycle time, *Then* we can launch products faster.
- *If* we launch our products faster, *Then* we increase market share.

Third, you can stack related Objectives into in a vertical hierarchy. The LogFrame matrix incorporates this visual format.

Increase market share
↑
Launch products faster
↑
Reduce production cycle time

Each of these three different language patterns is valuable during project design for refining and communicating your project hypothesis. Now, let us consider a wider choice of verbs so you can best express your project intentions.

Communicate in Words and Diagrams

Project design is a discovery process. As your project begins, keep an open mind about how to best state each Objective. At the beginning, Objectives are naturally fuzzy and ragged, suggesting a general intent or direction, without real clarity or specificity. They need refining.

Choose the Right Verb

To broaden your word choice, I have compiled a menu of over 150 action verbs taken from scores of strategic and project plans as shown in Figure 3.1. Choose the ones that "feel right." The best wording typically emerges after two or three iterations.

Try beginning each Objective—especially at the Purpose level—with slightly different verbs (e.g., improve, upgrade, enhance, and evolve) to see which one resonates best. As you continue digging, you will find an ah-ha moment when the perfect phrasing pops up. A pitch-perfect Purpose is meaningful, motivating, and achievable.

There is value in being able to design and communicate your thinking in both words or diagrams. Let us review how to go from one to another.

Translate Objectives Trees into Narrative Language

We covered how to turn single chains of Objectives into words, and vice versa. Now let us examine how to turn Objectives Trees into narrative form.

You can start your creative design process by sketching out an Objectives Tree as shown in Figure 3.2 to visualize the major pieces and how they relate to each other, and then putting it into plain English words.

You might start with a whiteboard creative exercise, jotting down objectives on sticky notes and moving them around until the design emerges. Then you can document the design with conventional language.

To convert Objectives Trees into narrative form for use in text documents, use connector words. In written form, the Objectives Tree in Figure 3.2 becomes:

We will increase sales by improving our marketing as well as enhancing product features. To do this, we will have to hire better marketers and update the skills of existing staff. Market research is necessary in order to determine what customers really want, and delivering may require product redesign as well as changes to our manufacturing process.

The ability to "translate" from trees to narrative (and vice versa) enables us to understand and communicate a strategy in ways that engage both verbal and visual brain processing capabilities.

Master Menu of Strategic Management Verbs

• Accelerate	• Direct	• Invent	• Resolve
• Accomplish	• Discover	• Investigate	• Respond
• Achieve	• Dispose	• Lead	• Reverse
• Activate	• Dissolve	• Launch	• Review
• Administer	• Document	• Link	• Revise
• Amplify	• Educate	• Maintain	• Revitalize
• Analyze	• Elevate	• Manage	• Revolutionize
• Apply	• Eliminate	• Market	• Roll out
• Assemble	• Encourage	• Maximize	• Satisfy
• Assess	• Enhance	• Merge	• Save
• Assist	• Enjoy	• Minimize	• Schedule
• Attain	• Enlarge	• Modify	• Search
• Begin	• Enlighten	• Obliterate	• Select
• Build	• Enlist	• Obtain	• Sell
• Certify	• Ensure	• Operate	• Simplify
• Change	• Envision	• Optimize	• Slow
• Commercialize	• Erase	• Organize	• Solve
• Compare	• Establish	• Outline	• Speed up
• Complete	• Evaluate	• Persuade	• Spin off
• Compute	• Examine	• Plan	• Stabilize
• Conduct	• Execute	• Predict	• Stop
• Consolidate	• Expand	• Prepare	• Store
• Construct	• Explain	• Prevent	• Streamline
• Convert	• Explore	• Produce	• Strengthen
• Convince	• Fabricate	• Program	• Structure
• Coordinate	• Facilitate	• Project	• Submit
• Create	• Finalize	• Promote	• Support
• Decide	• Identify	• Prove	• Survey
• Decrease	• Implement	• Provide	• Synthesize
• Deduce	• Improve	• Publicize	• Systematize
• Define	• Improvise	• Qualify	• Teach
• Deliver	• Incorporate	• Quantify	• Test
• Demonstrate	• Increase	• Recommend	• Train
• Design	• Initiate	• Reduce	• Transform
• Destroy	• Install	• Reengineer	• Understand
• Detect	• Institute	• Remediate	• Update
• Determine	• Institutionalize	• Report	• Upgrade
• Develop	• Integrate	• Reorganize	• Utilize
• Diagnose	• Introduce	• Research	• Validate
			• Verify

FIGURE 3.1   Schmidt Master Menu of Strategic Management Verbs

FIGURE 3.2   Improve Sales Objectives Tree

Convert Narrative Text into Objectives Trees

You can also do the reverse translation from narrative form to tree form. Start with existing documentation, such as a business case, project charter, scope of work, management memo, or even a conversation.

Go through the document with a highlighter to mark every Objective you can find by searching for verbs. In addition, look for key phrases and connector words that suggest cause-effect relationships, so that you can construct your tree. They may be missing, but implied.

Treat all initial objectives as if molded in soft clay rather than as cast in concrete. Do not hesitate to suggest doing something a little different from what was originally requested if you believe it to be beneficial. If you dive into the problem and notice inconsistencies or problems regarding what is required or what is possible—speak up!

Simple Project Logic and the Strategic Hypotheses

Every project strategy can be expressed using just four levels of logically linked Objectives: Goal, Purpose, Outcomes, and Inputs. There are clear differences among them, as defined in Figure 3.3.

Admittedly, the choice of words used to define each level may seem arbitrary, but the meaning attached to each word is definitely not. Each objective carries a particular and precise meaning.

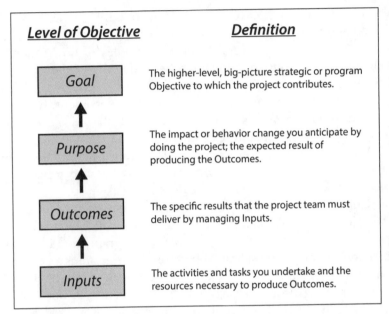

FIGURE 3.3 Definitions of the Four Levels of Objectives

Generic Format of the Simple Project Hypothesis

We have shown several examples of causally linked objectives; now here is the generic format for project design. Every project strategy can be summarized with this simple project hypothesis, reading from the bottom up.

- *If* we manage the Inputs, *Then* we can produce Outcomes.
- *If* we produce Outcomes, *Then* we will achieve an important Purpose.
- *If* we achieve a Purpose, *Then* we contribute to a valued Goal.

  Or expressed more succinctly:

- *If* Inputs, *Then* Outcomes.
- *If* Outcomes, *Then* Purpose.
- *If* Purpose, *Then* Goal.

You can think of these various Objectives as rungs on a ladder. The logic between levels is not random or accidental because each level forms a link in the causal chain. This causal logic permits a disciplined approach to project design.

Figure 3.4 shows several business examples of how these four levels summarize your strategic hypotheses. Figure 3.5 does the same with personal projects.

The LogFrame is meant to be a summary document. Keep your statement of Objectives short and easy to remember. Use the Success Measures column to expand upon them.

Words matter. Be consistent in using explicit definitions of project terms in order to reduce ambiguity. Just because something is labeled Goal, Purpose, or Outcome does not make it so.

Consider this phrase I found in a strategic plan: "The Goal of this project is to develop a safety training program." This is not correct. By our definition, the Goal of such a program would be "fewer accidents" or "increased safety." The training program is an Outcome because it is something the project team can make happen. "Develop a safety training program" may be the project name, but it is certainly not the Goal. The problem with labeling it a Goal is that a Goal is commonly understood to be the highest-level Objective. But by calling this the Goal, the underlying reason for the effort gets lost.

By focusing on the true Goal, the team can more easily craft a solution.

How Projects Deliver Benefits

The only reason we do projects is to produce measurable benefits for the organization, its customers, and/or its community. Those benefits could be a base of happy customers, better financial returns, a high-performing culture, or various other desired benefits. There is a clear distinction between *what is created* by a project and the *work done* to get there. Benefits occur and value is delivered at the Purpose and Goal levels, but the work occurs at the Input to Outcome levels, as shown in Figure 3.6.

Recognize the important distinction between Outcomes and Purpose. Outcomes are deliverables the project team can control, make happen, and be held accountable for delivering. Purpose is the expected impact from the deliverables, the aiming point beyond the team's direct control. Purpose is less certain to be reached than Outcomes.

Strategic Hypotheses – Business Examples

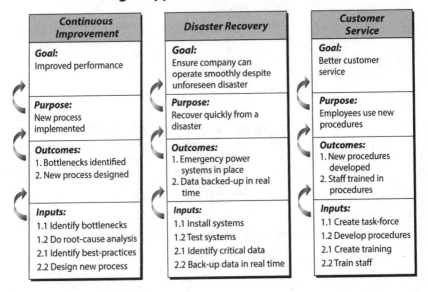

Continuous Improvement	Disaster Recovery	Customer Service
Goal: Improved performance	**Goal:** Ensure company can operate smoothly despite unforeseen disaster	**Goal:** Better customer service
Purpose: New process implemented	**Purpose:** Recover quickly from a disaster	**Purpose:** Employees use new procedures
Outcomes: 1. Bottlenecks identified 2. New process designed	**Outcomes:** 1. Emergency power systems in place 2. Data backed-up in real time	**Outcomes:** 1. New procedures developed 2. Staff trained in procedures
Inputs: 1.1 Identify bottlenecks 1.2 Do root-cause analysis 2.1 Identify best-practices 2.2 Design new process	**Inputs:** 1.1 Install systems 1.2 Test systems 2.1 Identify critical data 2.2 Back-up data in real time	**Inputs:** 1.1 Create task-force 1.2 Develop procedures 2.1 Create training 2.2 Train staff

FIGURE 3.4 Read from Bottom to Top using *If-Then* Language

Strategic Hypotheses – Personal Examples

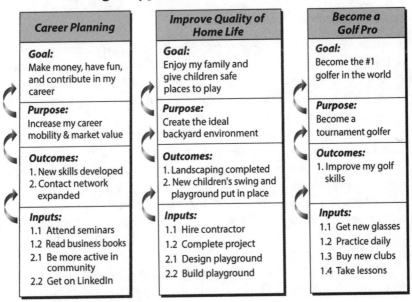

Career Planning	Improve Quality of Home Life	Become a Golf Pro
Goal: Make money, have fun, and contribute in my career	**Goal:** Enjoy my family and give children safe places to play	**Goal:** Become the #1 golfer in the world
Purpose: Increase my career mobility & market value	**Purpose:** Create the ideal backyard environment	**Purpose:** Become a tournament golfer
Outcomes: 1. New skills developed 2. Contact network expanded	**Outcomes:** 1. Landscaping completed 2. New children's swing and playground put in place	**Outcomes:** 1. Improve my golf skills
Inputs: 1.1 Attend seminars 1.2 Read business books 2.1 Be more active in community 2.2 Get on LinkedIn	**Inputs:** 1.1 Hire contractor 1.2 Complete project 2.1 Design playground 2.2 Build playground	**Inputs:** 1.1 Get new glasses 1.2 Practice daily 1.3 Buy new clubs 1.4 Take lessons

FIGURE 3.5 Read from Bottom to Top using *If-Then* Language

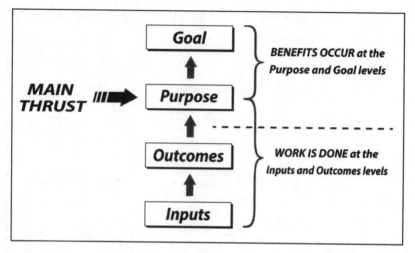

FIGURE 3.6 Work Done vs. Value Created

The Project leader's job is to deliver the set of Outcomes necessary to achieve Purpose. This requires clearly defining the Purpose, as well as the expected set of conditions (Success Measures) that signal project success. We will cover that further in Chapter 5.

Organize Your Project into Chunks

Chunking means breaking down something big (problem, strategy, goal) into smaller, more accessible "chunks" (such as phases, components, categories, and aspects, etc.) The word "chunk" doubles as a *verb* as well as *noun*. The verb expresses the thinking process, while the noun describes the resulting categories.

Project chunking begins when you first consider project phases. Most large, complex, or long-term projects consist of sequential or overlapping phases which break the project into manageable components. Phase chunking can occur in smaller projects, too.

Standard phase names exist for many types of projects, but if your project type has no standard phases, create your own. With a fuzzy project, Phase One might be "Problem Definition." Use whatever chunking criteria make the most sense in your project.

The most common first-order chunking logic is by phases, with secondary chunking logic in each phase. Decisions about project chunking are first made when you consider whether your LogFrame plan will cover the whole project, or just one part or phase.

Turn a Problem into Objectives

Every project is meant to solve a problem, improve a situation, or capture an opportunity. Before developing a solution, be clear about the problem you aim to solve as well as what solution methodology you will use.

Many widely accepted problem analysis methodologies are available, such as the Fishbone Analysis, the Five Why Questions, basic TQM tools, and Value Stream Mapping.

No matter which methodology you use, be sure to invest time in early problem identification and analysis to zero in on the problem you aim to solve. It is better to solve the right problem poorly than to solve the wrong problem well. And as Peter Drucker reminds us, *"There is surely nothing quite so useless as doing with great efficiency what should not be done at all."*

A problem is simply a project in disguise. Dig to find the root causes and the right problem to solve. Consult with stakeholders by asking questions such as the following:

- What do you see as the fundamental problem?
- Why is this a problem?
- What makes it a problem, and for whom?
- Who "owns" the problem? The solution?
- What are the root causes of the problem?
- What are the consequences if we ignore the problem?
- How will we know when we have solved the problem?

Take time to carefully diagnose the problem because the way you define the project shapes the scope and range of solution options.

Identify the Problem You Choose to Solve

A classic story told by the legendary systems thinker Russell Ackoff proves the point that unless you zoom in on the right problem, you risk solving the wrong problem. Let me share a classic story of just how that can happen.

Tenants in an aging 20-story Chicago office building complained about the long wait for elevators in the lobby. Maria, the owner of the building, became concerned her small number of business tenants would relocate to a newer space.

So, she hired a consulting engineer to solve the slow elevator problem. The elevator was too old for upgrading, so the consultant recommended a replacement elevator system. Maria gulped at the $300,000 price tag—fearing she could not increase rents to cover the cost without losing tenants.

Fortunately, Maria got a second opinion. Rather than automatically accepting the problem as "The elevators are too slow," this creative consultant suggested the real problem was "Tenants get bored while waiting." His recommended solution: Entertain and distract tenants so they would not mind the long wait.

Following his advice, Maria renovated the lobby, installed television monitors tuned to a comedy channel, and mounted mirrors by each elevator so people could preen themselves while waiting. This "jazzed-up lobby" solved the problem for just $30,000, which was 10 percent of the cost of the new elevator option. This solution satisfied the tenants, which delighted Maria. The dramatic savings were worth taking time to find the right Objective to address, instead of adopting the first solution that came to mind.

These two solutions in Figure 3.7 illustrate two different strategies to reach the same Goal.

Engage others in defining the core problems and potential Objectives from multiple perspectives. Remember: It is better to partially solve the right problem than to fully solve the wrong problem.

Solution #1 Objectives		Solution #2 Objectives	
Goal: Keep tenants happy		*Goal:* Keep tenants happy	
Purpose: Reduce wait time		*Purpose:* Keep tenants from boredom while waiting	
Outcomes: New elevator installed		*Outcomes:* Lobby renovated	
Inputs: Install elevator @ $300,000		*Inputs:* Install monitor and mirrors @ $30,000	

FIGURE 3.7 Two Alternate Solutions to Reach Goal

Review Key Points

1. A common language allows people from diverse backgrounds to communicate and contribute to project design. A genuine shared understanding of what the project is designed to accomplish will reduce later rework.

2. Follow this basic language formula for clear and well-formed Objectives: a well-chosen verb followed with a brief description of the Object.

3. Refer to the *Schmidt Master Menu of Strategic Management Verbs* to capture those just-right, on-the-mark phrases that resonate your true intentions.

4. Four levels of linked Objectives form the backbone of any project plan: Inputs, Outcomes, Purpose, and Goal. Each carries a different yet explicit meaning.

5. In general, project teams manage Inputs to produce Outcomes in order to accomplish a Purpose that contributes to a Goal. Work is done at the level of Inputs and Outcomes, but benefits occur at the Purpose and Goal levels.

6. Before deciding on a solution, be clear about what problem you are trying to solve.

7. Objectives received from a chain of command are not always well thought out. Do not treat them as commandments carved in stone. Offer alternatives where you see issues.

Coming Up Next

Now that we have set the stage by covering fundamental logic and language concepts, in the next chapter we will dive into how to use our principle power tool—the LogFrame—to lay out the *Who, What, Why, When,* and *How* of a project on a single page. We introduce *Four Critical Strategic Questions* that must be answered in sequential order to avoid the pitfalls many projects fall into. We will see why the LogFrame is called the "Swiss Army Knife" of Strategic Thinking because it adapts to multiple situations. We also cover how to add Assumptions to our logic to solidify our project strategy.

4

Exploring the Logical Framework Approach

Make no little plans; they have no magic to stir men's blood and probably will, themselves, not be realized. Make big plans; aim high in hope and work, remembering that a noble, logical diagram, once recorded, will never not die.

—Daniel H. Burnham, American architect and urban planner

Now that you have learned the underlying concepts of logic and language, let us apply them. This chapter explores how to use the LogFrame matrix and the Four Critical Strategic Questions to drive a solution. You will discover how the LogFrame acts as a higher-level design tool and synchronizes with a variety of project management tools that may already be in use.

A well-thought-out LogFrame can describe a project strategy on a single page for simple projects, and on three pages for a more complex one. For small and medium-size projects, this may be the only tool you need. For larger projects, it offers a wise starting point to be followed by applying other project tools and analytic techniques.

Whenever you see the phrase "develop a LogFrame," it means to be systematic and thorough in designing your project. The Log-Frame is simply a tool to help you do so.

The case study in this chapter looks at how an organization in deep trouble turned itself around.

Equip Leaders with Practical Tools

I vividly remember the dust, the smells, the chaos, and the confusion when I first landed in Dacca, Bangladesh. What a culture shock to travel from the affluent Georgetown neighborhood where I lived in Washington, D.C., to one of the poorest nations on the planet.

Bangladesh's main industry was agriculture. Millions of farmers with small plots of land did their best to grow food, but their methods were inefficient, and they did not produce enough to feed the fast-growing population.

My client was the Bangladesh Planning Commission, responsible for designing programs to increase agricultural production in order to reduce malnutrition and starvation. They had the responsibility and the commitment, but lacked the necessary planning skills and tools. My job was to train them. Before my trip, I sketched out the logic of my consulting help as this:

- *If* I create and deliver a quality training program, *Then* staff could be trained.
- *If* staff are trained, *Then* they would *use* the training to design effective programs.
- *If* they design effective programs, *Then* farmers can grow more food.

Applying LogFrame definitions, the logic becomes:

Goal = Farmers grow more food

↑

Purpose = Planning Commission staff *uses* new skills to design programs

↑

Outcomes = Planning Commission staff trained in project/program design

↑

Inputs = Create and deliver a quality training program

My ability to deliver results went only as far as trained staff (Outcome). Beyond that, it was up to the trained staff to *use* what they learned (Purpose) in order to achieve the Goal of more food.

After arriving in Bangladesh and getting to know the Planning Commission staff, we clarified the strategy behind the work *they* would perform.

- *If* we develop programs to train farmers, *Then* they will adopt better farming methods.
- *If* they adopt better methods, *Then* they will grow more food.
- *If* they grow more food, *Then* we can feed the people and avoid starvation.

In LogFrame terms, the four objectives are:

Goal = Feed the people and avoid starvation

↑

Purpose = Farmers grow more food

↑

Outcomes = Farmers adopt better farming methods

↑

Inputs = Develop strategies and programs to train farmers

This logic may have been obvious, but it had never been clearly stated in a way that allowed the staff to identify distinct measures for each level. Now, by collecting and analyzing the right data, they could test various approaches, track progress, and evaluate the impact of strategies.

Over a period of six weeks, we mapped out their major programs with Objectives Trees and key projects with LogFrames. I will always cherish what my Bengali counterpart said at the end of the project. *"Terry, your system is so clear that everyone from the Minister of Agriculture to the farmer in the field can get on the same page and understand their role in the project. You gave us exactly what we need to move forward."*

Life Lessons Learned

This project taught me three lifelong lessons. The first lesson is to not take food for granted in a world where well over a billion people are malnourished and live in extreme poverty.

The second lesson is that a common planning approach and simple tools can empower committed people to make a huge difference.

The third lesson is that a system thinking approach is necessary to identify and manage the web of cross-connecting relationships within, and extending beyond, any specific project. In this case, growing more food was *necessary* to feed the people, but not *sufficient* in itself. Feeding the people also required setting up other systems to collect harvested rice from the fields, distribute it to where it is needed, and more.

Your own projects exist in a larger web of relationships as well. They impact and are impacted by factors external to your project, which you clearly need to consider. By understanding these relationships, you boost the chances for your project to be a real winner.

Examine the LogFrame Structure and Questions

The LogFrame design process guides you in thinking through all the critical issues as you develop solutions. A summary of the project information captured in each LogFrame cell is shown in Figure 4.1.

As NASA Rule #15 reminds us, effective initial planning is absolutely vital.

Objectives	Success Measures	Verification	Assumptions
Goal: ▶ Big-Picture Objective to which Project Purpose contributes	**Goal Measures:** Measures of Goal Achievement (quality, quantity, time)	Data sources to monitor and verify Goal	**To reach Goal:** External conditions needed to reach Goal and beyond
Purpose: ▶ Change expected from producing Outcomes ▶ Motivation for Project	**Purpose Measures:** Success conditions expected at end of Project (quality, quantity, time)	Data sources to monitor and verify Purpose	**To achieve Purpose:** External conditions needed to achieve Purpose
Outcomes: ▶ Specific Results expected from Project Team ▶ What good managers can make happen	**Outcome Measures:** Description of completed Outcomes (quality, quantity, time)	Data sources to monitor and verify Outcomes	**To produce Outcomes:** External conditions needed to produce Outcomes
Inputs: ▶ Activities and Responsibilities needed to produce Outcomes	**Input Measures:** Resource Budget and Schedule	Data sources to monitor and verify Inputs	**To obtain and manage Inputs:** External conditions necessary to obtain and manage Inputs

FIGURE 4.1 Definitions of Terms in the LogFrame Matrix

Using the LFA for initial planning accomplishes many of the same objectives found in other Project Management methodologies, but in a much simpler way.

This approach meshes nicely with the knowledge areas and five process groups, which have been carefully crafted by the Project Management Institute (PMI). In their certification program, PMI emphasizes the careful systems thinking that links Initiation to Planning, to Executing, to Monitoring and Controlling, and finally to Closing.

Notice how each of these Process Groups feeds logically on the results of the upfront strategic planning put into place by the Log-Frame and its four questions. The first two processes (Initiation and Planning) are the most critical in getting projects off the ground, and that's where this approach shines. It is clear that starting with the Logical Framework gives strength and meaning to the Project Charter, which is generally considered the starting point for a project.

One user observed "this approach provides 80 percent of the value of the more complex processes with just 20 percent of the work." Eighty percent is usually enough to get going, and you will discover what else you need once you get started.

Every LogFrame reflects a particular perspective or scope. This perspective can be on a program or on a single project. It can also focus on just one Outcome within a project. The scope can even be national in impact, as a later case study shows.

From any perspective or frame of reference, the same *Why-What-How* construct logically links Objectives together remains true. In that sense, the LogFrame is fractal in nature. By fractal, we mean that whether the perspective is micro or macro in scope, the same principles apply.

Four Critical Strategic Questions Drive the Solution

Getting the right answers begins by asking the right questions. The LogFrame features a question-driven discovery process. I have crafted these *Four Critical Strategic Questions* to guide you. As shown in Figure 4.2, they are simple questions—that's the point. I believe it

Objectives	Success Measures	Verification	Assumptions
Goal			
Purpose			
Outcomes			
Inputs			

☐ *1. What are we trying to accomplish and why?*

▨ *2. How will we measure success?*

▮ *3. What other conditions must exist?*

▢ *4. How do we get there?*

FIGURE 4.2 Four Critical Strategic Questions

was Einstein who said if you cannot explain something in simple language, you do not understand it well enough.

The answers to these Four Critical Strategic Questions drive the project design, and their answers populate the matrix cells:

1. **What Are We Trying to Accomplish and Why? (Objectives)**
   The first column describes Objectives and the *If-Then* logic linking them together. The LogFrame makes important distinctions among various "levels" of Objectives: strategic intention (Goal), project impact (Purpose), project deliverables (Outcomes), and the key action steps (Inputs).

2. **How Will We Measure Success? (Measures and Verifications)**
   The second column identifies the Measures of success for each Objective at each level. Here you select appropriate Measures and choose quantity, quality, and time indicators to clarify what each Objective means. The third column summarizes how to verify the status of each of the Measures at each level.

3. **What Other Conditions Must Exist? (Assumptions)**
   The fourth column captures Assumptions: those ever-present, but often neglected risk factors outside of the project, on which project success depends. Defining and testing Assumptions lets you spot potential problems and deal with them in advance.

4. **How Do We Get There? (Inputs)**
   The bottom row summarizes the implementation plan: *Who* does *What*, *When*, and with what resources. Conventional project management tools like Work Breakdown Structures (WBS) and Gantt chart schedules fit here.

These carefully crafted questions add significant value in virtually any situation when addressed in that order. Often, the first three are glossed over. But starting a journey before knowing where you want to be risks ending up somewhere else.

How a Stalled Team Finally Got Going

The call came from Keith, an Information Technology (IT) manager who had attended my strategy workshops at UCLA Extension's

Technical Management Program. His task force was launching a critical initiative, but their planning was bogged down.

After several frustrating meetings with little progress, Keith invited me to facilitate their next one. While Keith was familiar with the LogFrame, the others were not. People often resist what they do not understand, so I decided to let a project design take shape through natural conversation, using the four questions as springboards, but without first presenting the matrix, which can look intimidating until it is explained.

From the start, I watched a dozen frustrated task force members from several departments argue the merits of *How* to do the project using different software solutions and other technical issues. But it was obvious they had no shared understanding of the *Why* behind the project. Then a grumpy-looking executive glared at me and asked, "Okay, you're the consultant. We're stuck. What should we do?"

I responded by tossing out this first question.

What are We Trying to Accomplish and Why?

The executive looked at Keith and his team looked at each other as if to say, "For the money we are paying this guy, we expected a brilliant answer, not a simple question."

But this question shifted the discussion from technical solutions to customer needs, stakeholders, expectations, and operational benefits. As their answers tumbled out, I captured them on a whiteboard. It did not take them long to conclude the Goal was to deliver customer value.

While hardly profound, this question is the place to start, whatever your issue. *Why* the project needs to be done deserves deep attention because those answers drive everything else. Without being clear about the *Why* and *What* the project must deliver, it is easy to get lost in the technical jungle of *How*.

When Keith's team reached a consensus, I wrote the word OBJECTIVES in capital letters on the whiteboard, and I listed their Objectives in a hierarchy, with the Goal at the top, Purpose and Outcomes below, and with vertical arrows connecting them. With our project hypothesis beginning to take shape, I asked the next question.

How will We Measure Success?

Their facial expressions suggested I had revealed some magic formula unlocking the universe. Actually, this unlocks the meaning behind each Objective. Finally, a team member spoke up, "Our Goal is to deliver customer value; so, is not it clear what constitutes success?"

No. That's too general and vague. They then began identifying how they would measure success of each Objective, using performance indicators and numerical targets.

This question seldom gets the attention it deserves. It's easy to presume the answer must be either obvious, or "some other department," will decide. However, until you define how success is measured, it's not clear what each Objective really means. I wrote down the heading word MEASURES on the board, and added the measures they mentioned next to each Objective.

I also added the heading VERIFICATION on the board, and listed the data sources and methods to track each Measure.

As we sketched out Success Measures for those Objectives, the atmosphere in the room changed. Progress was now being made, and the worry lines on Keith's brow softened.

When I posed the next question, out of the corner of my eye, I caught a smile breaking out on my glaring/grumpy executive.

What Other Conditions Must Exist?

In other words, what are the risks, and how can they be handled? They shared concerns such as training, meshing with existing systems, dependencies, related projects, technology issues, resource issues, and other important considerations.

PMI and other project organizations place a great deal of emphasis on early risk identification and require you to have risk mitigation plans so you can identify precursors to risk events. Having the risks identified early using LogFrame is a huge advantage. Defining Assumptions is the jumping-off point to more extensive risk analysis.

I added these Assumptions to our in-progress project design under the heading ASSUMPTIONS. Then I drew lines between the columns and horizontal lines across each level, leaving the bottom row blank. Voilà, a LogFrame is emerging! They were impressed by what they accomplished.

They created a solid project foundation based on their collective experience and common sense. Now we could finally turn the technical people loose to fight over the nitty-gritty details. That was their job to complete. Time for the next question.

How do We Get There?

Far too many project teams dive deep into a task and schedule analysis much too soon, or they get sidelined by premature technical arguments. Ensure you get the maximum benefits from the fourth question by asking it last in the sequence.

These Four Critical Strategic Questions form the heart of Strategic Project Management. Each should be asked and answered in this order. Of course, the questions are iterative and interconnected. Best practice is to give first-cut answers and cycle through them several times, each time sharpening your plan and improving your confidence in the strategy.

Answers to these questions—and secondary questions they will stimulate—will guide you in putting the puzzle pieces together in a structured and logical way. And just as in a crossword puzzle, as you add additional connections, your "project solution" will begin to emerge from your data, analysis, and experience.

Strengthen Your Project Design

Projects are risky. Before committing resources, you want to be reasonably confident that your approach will achieve the desired Objectives. That means examining the main risk elements and dealing with them.

The simple *If-Then* logic construct presumes that one level leads to another, but are you reasonably sure, or is this just wishful thinking?

That's where Assumptions come in. You can begin risk reduction by identifying certain Assumptions that must be valid. Assumptions are defined as necessary conditions for success, which are largely outside your control or the scope of the project.

Assumptions Expand and Complete the Hypothesis

To have confidence in the project design, we must define, at each level, all the *necessary and sufficient* conditions to reach the next level. These conditions include both the *hypotheses* and the *Assumptions*. Project hypotheses are internal to the project and reflect our view of cause-effect, while Assumptions are external.

The concept of Assumptions (risk) forces us to expand our original hypotheses to reflect uncertainties outside of our logic chain. The enriched logic becomes "*If-And-Then*" logic, as diagrammed in Figure 4.3. I call this *The Implementation Equation*™.

By incorporating Assumptions, in the right-most column of the LogFrame, the flow of our design logic looks like Figure 4.4.

By carefully considering Assumptions during the design phase, the project design will be stronger, and the team can anticipate the kind of difficulties that might arise during implementation.

The Implementation Equation™

▶ *If* Inputs *And* valid Assumptions, *Then* Outcomes

▶ *If* Outcomes *And* valid Assumptions, *Then* Purpose

▶ *If* Purpose *And* valid Assumptions, *Then* Goal

FIGURE 4.3   The Implementation Equation™

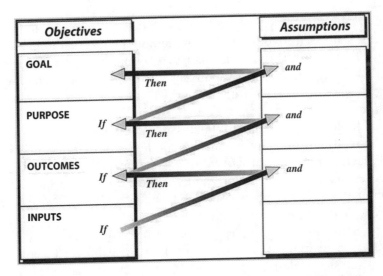

FIGURE 4.4   If / AND / Then Logic Completes the Hypothesis

Evaluate Your Assumptions

Just because you state an Assumption does not make it true, as plenty of failed projects show. Every Assumption requires up-close inspection with a skeptical magnifying glass. Ask the following of each one:

- Is this Assumption reasonable? What are the odds it is valid? How do we know?
- What are the consequences for the project if it's not valid? How severe is the impact?
- How can we influence the Assumption in our favor?

Since Assumptions shine a bright light on possible pitfalls in our climb up the causal hierarchy, the benefit of spotting them early should be immediately apparent. Better to catch these potential dealbreakers upfront and decide how to handle them then rather than pay lip-service and have them sabotage you later. Chapter 7 covers how to analyze Assumptions and reduce preventable risks.

Think from Multiple Perspectives

The organization power of the LogFrame derives from how it incorporates features from other planning methodologies and disciplines.

Think of the LogFrame matrix as a superstructure, an overarching bridge that draws upon several other valuable methodologies whose principles are incorporated into the matrix, as shown in Figure 4.5.

The LogFrame structure invites, accommodates, and incorporates virtually any other useful analytic method. For example, financial tools such as *Return on Investment (ROI)* and *Benefit/cost analysis* apply when estimating the economic value of the Purpose and Goal. And looking closely, we see how concepts from *Total Quality Management* and *Six Sigma* appear in multiple cells.

Finally, and most important, the LogFrame speeds up *Team Building* by giving a structure for people to collaborate to create a sound and shared design.

When teams flesh out their LogFrame with tools such as online team canvas software or a whiteboard, it's remarkable how

The LogFrame Incorporates Multiple Perspectives

The Logical Framework is a Systems Thinking "meta-framework"
that incorporates several other useful methodologies
into an interactive visual matrix. These include:

Scientific Method – *a project strategy can be organized as a testable hypothesis using causal logic. Execution tests the validity of the hypothesis.*

Strategic Planning – *begin from future vision, goals, and positioning, then derive projects. Goals and Purpose-level Objectives capture strategic intent.*

Project Management – *focuses on turning activities and resources into Outcomes or deliverables. Input tools cover budgets, schedules and roles.*

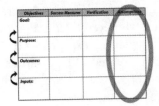

Risk Management – *outside factors always exist; identify and test your assumptions. This column is the jumping off point for more rigorous risk analysis and mitigation.*

Management by Objectives – *project objectives must be measurable and verifiable. Setting clear measures in advance simplifies monitoring and evaluation.*

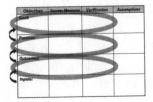

Agile – *the stories within any sprint contribute to specific Outcomes.*

FIGURE 4.5   The LogFrame Blends Together Multiple Perspectives

much more productive and creative they become. Try it and find out for yourself.

Applications of this approach are virtually endless. This same thought process applies not just to work projects, but to personal ones as well. More about this in Chapter 12. For now, let's walk through a case study of how the LogFrame helped guide a solution to a big problem.

Even though the subject matter of this case may be very different from your own work, you will see how the framework helps you create effective solutions to big problems.

Case Study: Managing Enterprise-Wide Change

There was serious trouble at the Fircrest School for the developmentally disabled.

Fircrest School is a Seattle residential home for some 800 adults and children who suffer from serious mental, physical, and emotional developmental disabilities. It is funded by both the State of Washington and the federal government and is managed by the Washington State Department of Social and Health Services.

These are difficult and dangerous places to work, and the staff was overwhelmed. There were several unexplained injuries to residents and even one suspicious death, which triggered a federal audit.

The federal audit was performed by visiting experts who discovered residents were not being properly treated. They witnessed an overuse of psychoactive medications and restraints. Quality assurance was lacking. Medical and nursing care records were not timely or accurate. Too many nurses were assigned to administrative duties and too few to resident care and treatments.

After the audit, certification was revoked, along with millions of dollars of federal funding. This presented Fircrest management with serious problems that needed to be solved quickly and in the right way. Project Manager Katie Cameron used the LogFrame with her project team to develop a solution strategy.

They used a simple technique to get started. The team identified aspects of the problems and their symptoms. These were then inverted to generate their draft Objectives, providing a pool of possibilities to work with.

Problem/Symptoms	Objectives
People getting injured ————→	Reduce or eliminate injuries
Too much use of restraints ————→	Less use of restraints
Poor quality assurance ————→	Improve quality assurance
Inaccurate medical records ————→	Improve records accuracy
Too many nurses doing admin work →	Assign more nurses to care

After careful consideration and discussion, they stated the Goal and Purpose as shown below:

Goal: Federal certification standards are achieved and maintained at Fircrest School.

Purpose: People who live at Fircrest are safe, healthy, receive quality care, and their human rights are protected.

Quick Quiz: Before we continue, how might you measure this Purpose statement? What specific indicators would you choose to capture the meaning of words like "safe," "healthy," "quality care," and "human rights"? Take a moment to consider. I will wait . . .

The Purpose statement the Fircrest team developed is shown in Figure 4.6, along with Measures and Means of Verification. While this statement contains many parts that need to be measured, targeted indicators are identified for the key words in the Purpose. These, along with the Verification method listed in the third column, were sufficient to evaluate project success.

They went on to identify a set of six Outcomes they believed were necessary to solve the problems, provide high-quality care, and get certified. Figure 4.7 on pages 66 to 68 shows their complete LogFrame.

Objectives	Success Measures	Verification
Purpose:	**End of Project Status:**	
People who live at Fircrest are safe and healthy, receive quality care, and their human rights are protected.	1. A 50% reduction in resident injuries that require nursing or medical care (or other intervention) occurs between 1/1 and 10/31.	1.1 Review and summarize incident reports. 1.2 Review and tabulate injuries from medical notes.
	2. No unusual or suspicious resident deaths occur between 1/1 and 10/31.	2. Review coroner reports
	3. An 80% reduction in restraints and time out use will be achieved between 1/1 and 10/31.	3. Review and summarize restraint and time out records.
	4. A 25% reduction in number of residents being prescribed psychoactive medication occurs between 1/1 and 10/31.	4. Review pharmacy and drug administrative records.
	5. 75% of residents are engaged in paid work activities for three more hours per day by 9/1.	5. Collect, review and summarize resident production records and paycheck information.

FIGURE 4.6   Fircrest Purpose, Success Measures, and Verifications

Review the Fircrest LogFrame

This case study reflects a highly effective use of LogFrame design concepts by the team. As you take time to review it, note the following features.

Brevity and Clarity

A complex project was captured on just three pages. Often one page will suffice.

Sound Logic

The Purpose and Goal are well-stated, with a clear logical relationship between them. The Purpose statement expresses the transformed conditions required and expected by producing the Outcomes.

Meaningful Measures

The Purpose Measures spell out in advance the necessary data needed for later evaluation of Purpose-level impact, while the Verification column shows how data would be gathered.

Well-Chunked Outcomes

The six Outcomes seem appropriate, necessary, and sufficient to achieve their Purpose. They are described clearly enough that everyone could understand how the various pieces fit together.

Organized Inputs

The implementation plan was summarized in a Gantt chart. The number of input tasks is not overwhelming. Note also how the task numbering relates directly to the corresponding Outcome.

Key Assumptions Identified

These cover such factors as internal risks, data-quality issues, and actions required by outside entities such as the Attorney General. By following this design, and making adjustments along the way, the Fircrest team improved and achieved the Purpose of the care provided and regained certification.

Is It Good Enough?

LogFrames do not have to be perfect to be useful. The best measures of the LogFrame's usefulness are what quality guru J. Duran said: *fitness for use*. The bonus materials include a quality checklist you can use to evaluate and strengthen your project designs.

Logical Framework for
Improving Social Service Delivery (Fircrest School for the Developmentally Disabled)

Objectives	Success Measures	Verification	Assumptions
Goal: Federal certification standards are achieved and maintained at Fircrest School.	**Goal Measures:** 1. Sometime after October 31, all ICF/MR regulatory surveys will be completed with no findings of conditional level deficiencies. 2. Fircrest continues to operate at high standards of health, safety, quality care and human rights.	1. Written decision from survey team with no conditional level findings. 2. Follow-up annual surveys with no negative findings.	**Assumptions to reach Goal:** 1. DSHS Secretary does not make agreement with government that Fircrest is unaware of. 2. No unanticipated Federal government (Dept. of Justice) litigation actions. 3. State Attorney General will have plan in place to file appeal by 8/3.
Purpose: People who live at Fircrest are safe, healthy, receive quality care and their human rights are protected.	**Purpose Measures:** 1. A 50% reduction in resident injury that requires nursing, medical care or intervention occurs between 1/1 and 10/31. 2. No unusual or suspicious resident deaths occur between 1/1 and 10/31. 3. An 80% reduction in restraints and time out use will be achieved between 1/1 and 10/31. 4. A 25% reduction in number of residents being prescribed psychoactive medication occurs between 1/1 and 10/31. 5. 75% of residents are engaged in paid work activities for three or more hours per day by 9/1.	1.1 Review and summarize incident reports. 1.2 Review/tabulate injuries from medical notes. 2. Review coroner reports. 3. Review and summarize restraint and time out records. 4. Review pharmacy/drug administration records. 5. Collect, review and summarize resident production records and paycheck information.	**Assumptions to achieve Purpose:** 1. Resident injuries are all reported on incident reports and progress notes. 2. Coroner conducts autopsies on all deaths. 3. Staff fill out restraint/time out records. 4. Production records are kept with sufficient detail.

FIGURE 4.7 Improving Social Service Delivery

Objectives	Success Measures	Verification	Assumptions
Outcomes: 1. New resident rehabilitation program system is implemented. 2. Quality Assurance system is implemented to maintain rehabilitation program changes. 3. Facility reorganized with staff redeployed. 4. Human rights protection is implemented. 5. Medical and nursing care records are streamlined to free up more MD and nurse treatment hours. 6. Physical plant "beautification" and modifications to support new programs are completed.	**Outcome Measures:** 1.1 By July 1, 95% of resident (awake) hours will be organized and managed by new treatment programs. 2.1 At least 10 FTEs are assigned to conduct QA activities. 2.2 QA checklist with target program indicators is implemented in all training locations. 2.3 QA data is used by program teams to modify/revise/correct faulty programs. 3.1 By June 1, 100% of affected staffing change will be completed. Staff better deployed to support resident care and treatment. 4.1 100% of resident behavior programs and 100% of prescribed psychoactive medications have consent from legal representative by 9/1. 4.2 By September 1, 80% of resident-initiated grievances will be recognized/responded to by at least one protection committee member within 48 hours. 4.3 An ombudsman is available for residents and families by June 15. 5.1 By June 15, new medical record forms are in 100% of resident charts and are being completed accurately. 5.2 By September 1, at least 85% of nurses and MDs will increase treatment hours by 20%. 6.1 1000 square feet of a new day program space is created by June 1. 6.2 New living room furniture and furnishings will be in place in 28 houses by August 1. 6.3 All campus lawns are cut to "acceptable" level and maintained on weekly basis, beginning May 1.	1.1 Observe each hour of program at each training site. 2.1 Check personnel records. 2.2 Checklist published. 2.3 Survey all program teams for use of data. 3.1 Check personnel records. 4.1 Records reviewed. 4.2 Minutes reviewed. 4.3 Appointments announced. 5.1 Sample 25% of records. 5.2 Nurses and MDs will conduct one week of self-survey/work-time study. 6.1 Tour and measure space. 6.2 Tour all homes. 6.3 Spot check weekly.	**Assumptions to produce Outcomes:** 1. Staff are adequately trained and aware of new program expectations. 2. Union agreement can be reached. 3. Chosen leading indicators are accurate reflections of good programs from the perspective of the survey team members. 4. Forms and records changes selected will result in "real" rather than "perceived" time savings for targeted personnel. 5. Maintenance man-hours and funding available. 6. Budget authorized.

FIGURE 4.7 Continued

Inputs:	How team will produce Outcomes		Schedule (in months)	Assumptions for Inputs:
	Action Steps	**Responsible**	**$** J F M A M J J A S O N D	
1.	**NEW RESIDENT REHABILITATION PROGRAMS**		$60K	1. QA System/data can be computerized
1.1	Retain technical experts	Director		
1.2	Develop schedule	Expert		2. Computer staff have expertise to design adequate system
1.3	Retrain staff	Expert		
1.4	Write new resident programs	Staff		
1.5	Implement and modify new programs as needed	Staff		
2.	**QUALITY ASSURANCE SYSTEM**		$25K	3. Union agreement reached
2.1	Assign staff	Superintndnt		4. Sufficient volunteers and non-staff committee members can be appointed
2.2	Design system	Expert		
2.3	Purchase computers	Bus. Mgr.		
2.4	Create prototype	QA Team		
2.5	Collect QA data	QA Team		
2.6	Distribute QA data	QA Team		
3.	**REORGANIZATION**			
3.1	New/changed roles and responsibilities determined	Expert		
3.2	Roles matched to job classes	Personnel		
3.3	Resources for new roles determined	Superintndnt		
3.4	Negotiate with unions	Superintndnt		
3.5	Notify affected staff	Personnel		
3.6	Staff practice new roles	Staff		
4.	**HUMAN RIGHTS SYSTEM**			
4.1	Write policy/procedure	Expert		
4.2	Establish new committees	Superintndnt		
4.3	Appoint committee members	Superintndnt		
4.4	Analyze QA data	Chair		
4.5	Review with Superintendent	Chair		
5.	**MEDICAL RECORDS**		$3K	
5.1	Identify target records	Expert		
5.2	Draft new forms and chart contents	Records		
5.3	Change forms/reprint new forms	Records		
5.4	Retrain staff	Staff		
5.5	Purge and revise charts	Staff		
6.	**PHYSICAL PLANT MODIFICATIONS**		$500K	
6.1	Design new program space	Staff		
6.2	Determine furniture requirements	Staff		
6.3	Purchase materials and furnishings	Bus. Mgr.		
6.4	Remodel/construct	Plant Mgr.		
6.5	Install new furnishings	Plant Mgr.		
6.6	Grounds maintenance scheduled implemented	Plant Mgr.		
		$ Total	**$588K**	

FIGURE 4.7   Continued

Review Key Points

1. The LogFrame is an effective planning method whether you are doing simple project planning with a specific Goal in mind; more complex planning when the end result is unclear; or when you reassess, readjust, and pivot your business.

2. The LogFrame incorporates features from multiple other planning methodologies and can enhance the effectiveness of other planning tools.

3. The Four Critical Strategic Questions offer a simple way to learn and leverage the concepts of the LogFrame and to design sound projects. Answers to these four questions, and subsequent questions they prompt, help to identify your important issues.

4. Goal is the big-picture *Why* and Purpose is the project-specific *Why*. Outcomes are *what* must be produced to achieve the Purpose. Inputs are the *How*, *Who*, and *When*: the tasks and resources required to achieve the Outcomes.

5. Assumptions are those conditions required for valid logic but are out of your control. They are brought into the LogFrame by using The Implementation Equation™. Assumptions are where the hidden risks are located. Identify and deal with them early and continually.

6. Purpose is the most critical Objective to focus on, as it describes the behavioral changes or conditions desired and required by delivering the Outcomes.

Coming Up Next

Part II of the book takes a deep dive into each of the four Strategic Questions, beginning with the first question in Chapter 5. The answer to that question identifies *Why* the project is being done, *What* it aims to achieve, and what impact it is expected to have. The difference between Goal and Purpose is explained, along with why Purpose is the most critical Objective to identify clearly and specifically, as it forms the design focus.

You will learn the importance of beginning with a clear hypothesis and detailed understanding of *Why* the project is needed before planning *How* to accomplish it. A Minimum Viable Project (MVP) can be defined by choosing the minimum set of Outcomes necessary and sufficient to achieve your initial Purpose.

Part II

Mastering the Four Critical Strategic Questions

In Part II, we expand on each of the four strategic questions and show how the answers populate the LogFrame matrix. Each question and answer provides a piece of the project puzzle solution.

- *Chapter 5* explores *Question #1*—Asking *What* results we are trying to accomplish and *Why* guides you in building a strong foundation.
- *Chapter 6* addresses Question #2—Asking *How* to measure success assists you in pinning down *What* each Objective means. Being able to describe what success looks like in advance grounds your project in the real world and shapes agreement.
- *Chapter 7* answers *Question #3*—Asking what other conditions must exist leads you to identify and reduce risk by evaluating your Assumptions.
- *Chapter 8* discusses *Question #4*—Asking *How* we get there is where you develop your execution plan, whether you follow a predictive or adaptive (agile) project lifecycle.

Use these questions as discussion springboards. They get the ball rolling and will spark secondary questions that deepen your conversation. Answering these key questions accomplishes the corresponding project design steps as shown in Figure II.1.

Questions Drive the Design Steps

Strategic Questions	Design Steps
1. What are we aiming to accomplish and why?	1. Define and align project Objectives
2. How will we measure success?	2. Select indicators and set targets
3. What other conditions must exist?	3. Surface Assumptions and reduce risks
4. How do we get there?	4. Lay out action plans – who, what, and when

FIGURE II.1   Four Strategic Questions; Four Project Design Steps

5

Question #1—What Are We Trying to Accomplish and Why?

Management by objectives works—if you know the objectives.
Ninety percent of the time you do not.

—Peter Drucker

Objectives	Success Measures	Verification	Assumptions
Goal			
Purpose			
Outcomes			
Inputs			

FIGURE 5.1   The Objectives Column Summarizes Your Project Hypothesis

Define and Align Key Objectives

The most vital planning step in any project is to be clear about *Why* you are doing it.

Beginning with *Why* gives you a higher and broader perspective. It is like hovering above a maze in a helicopter to more clearly see your solution path through the course. But if you stay at the ground level—the tasks—and have not seen a map of the maze, you will encounter more dead ends.

By understanding the *Why*, you can then apply your expertise to determine *What* the team must produce or deliver.

Defining and aligning your key Objectives builds a defensible business case and demonstrates why your idea is worthy of support. This means revisiting the Objectives column of the LogFrame matrix, as shown in Figure 5.1.

This chapter explores project design logic, and shares several application examples. It begins with a historic example of a very ambitious *Why*. If you are above a certain age, you will remember this event. If not, this first-person account of a proud moment in American history illustrates the power of a very big *Why*.

Let's Go to the Moon!

By the time John F. Kennedy became president in January 1961, the United States was still behind in the Cold War with the Soviet Union. And it did not escape the attention of the U.S. military that Russia's beach-ball-sized *Sputnik* satellite was designed to carry an atomic weapon that could be detonated over the U.S. mainland. America had no similar capability. Nor did it have any defense. That stimulated both a military and civilian rocket development program.

Then-president John F. Kennedy understood the critical need to capture the hearts and energy of Americans to close this gap. Protecting America was the ultimate Goal, but not one big enough to generate the excitement and focus he knew was needed. He needed a bigger Vision to inspire action. A few weeks later, Kennedy announced that Vision in a way to engage Americans' sense of adventure and competitiveness.

> In summary, Kennedy said this: "I commit this nation to landing a man on the moon and returning him safely before the end of this decade."

Notice the compact clarity of these 21 words and how they reflect key elements of the LogFrame. They summarize the primary Objective (land on the moon), which is adequately measured using Quality (alive), Quantity (at least one person), and Time (end of the current decade). As we will cover in Chapter 6, those three factors ("QQT") are the minimum required measures to spell out what an Objective means.

The strategic logic behind the moon program was:

- *If* we build a rocket and train astronauts, *Then* we can put men on moon.
- *If* we put men on moon, *Then* we can demonstrate superiority of Western systems.
- *If* we demonstrate superiority of Western systems, *Then* we can win the Cold War.
- And *If* we can win the Cold War, *Then* American families will be safer.

In addition to the safety Vision, landing a man on the moon would advance technology and bring significant international prestige.

At the time of Kennedy's declaration, no one knew exactly how this lunar landing Vision, this Super-Goal, would be achieved. But the Vision was crystal clear, and the mission mattered. This set into action a national program, the scope of which had never been seen before, involving over 160,000 people and 1,500 companies working together in a unified effort to develop an extraordinarily complex system of systems.

Why is this example significant? First, it reminds us of what people can do when they have a clear and compelling mission. Second, it illustrates that behind every project stands a series of higher-level strategic objectives. You might be surprised how often these may not be obvious to those doing the work. Third, this undertaking exemplifies program and project management at its finest. NASA borrowed best management practices from industry, and then improved and expanded them to cover the breadth of this program. The LogFrame's antecedents can be traced back to some of the strategic management tools, systems, and processes used for the moon program and throughout industry.

Countdown to Lift-Off

It was a few weeks before the expected launch of *Apollo 11* on July 19, 1969, and I was determined to be on the beach among the two million people expected to witness this historic lift-off. As a fresh college grad, cash was low, but determination was high, so I hitchhiked most of this 2,584-mile journey with a sleeping bag, $80 in my pocket, and a boatload of optimism.

I got an idea along the way and stopped at the NASA Press Office in Huntsville, AL. "Any chance of getting a press pass?"

This was the hottest media event of the century, and every major newspaper and magazine in the world was already on board. When they stopped laughing, I asked, "Is the *Helix* on your list?"

"The *Helix*? No. Are you their reporter?" I was not about to tell them the *Helix* was Seattle's local underground "hip-rag" that covered rock concerts, psychedelics, and free love.

"No, not at the moment, but I will be soon." Then I called the *Helix* editor to ask if they could use a reporter for the moon shot.

"Far out, man," he replied, sounding like he was already floating somewhere in outer space. I arrived at the Cape Kennedy Press Office hoping the editor had returned from Mars long enough to send the credentials. Yes! I was in!

Perusing the bushy gardens behind the Hilton for a place to pitch my sleeping bag, I noticed the sign: CBS PRIVATE EVENT: PRESS ONLY. This looked promising. I ditched the bag, dusted off my jeans, clipped on my press badge shown in Figure 5.2, and marched right in to feast on the most scrumptious buffet east of the Mississippi River.

As luck would have it, there was an empty seat right next to CBS's television anchor Walter Cronkite, known as "the most trusted man in America." Cronkite was as gracious as he was famous.

We talked about the historic journey into the unknown about to unfold and the courage and commitment it took to think boldly. We discussed the geopolitical stakes and the tremendous risks. So much could go so very badly, in front of 600 million people who would watch worldwide. But, yes, there are some risks worth taking because the benefits are worth it.

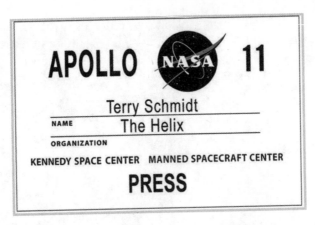

FIGURE 5.2   Press Badge for Accredited Reporters

The evening before launch, the press was escorted to the base of the majestic 363-foot high *Saturn V* rocket and its massive F1 engines that would generate 7.5 million pounds of thrust, enough power to get 3,100 tons of rocket and humans off the ground and on to their destiny. It may be a cliché, but it was a spiritual moment for me, and I still get goose bumps.

Before dawn, on launch day, I was sitting in the fifth row of the wooden press bleachers along with reporters from such notable publications as *Time*, *Le Monde*, the *New York Times*, and of course, the *Helix*! The blaring loudspeaker announcements all but drowned out the chirping frogs and the clackety-clacking of mechanical typewriters and reporters chattering in 33 different languages. See Figure 5.3.

You could feel the tension building as the countdown continued. One hour to go. Thirty minutes. One minute. The last 10 seconds. . .

10-9-8-7-6 (ignition) . . . the first stage engines roared to life, spewing fire and smoke like a thousand angry dragons.

5-4-3-2-1. . . lift off . . . The clamps flew open, and *Apollo 11* majestically rose off the earth and thundered into history. Its pulsating engines shook the air so hard that my palm trembled as I pointed it towards the rocket over two miles away. See Figure 5.4.

Four days later, Neil Armstrong stepped on the moon and reported "the Eagle has landed."

The Apollo program stands as testimony to what a committed team can accomplish when there is a compelling vision backed by

FIGURE 5.3   The International Press Awaiting Lift off

FIGURE 5.4   Lift-Off of *Apollo 11*

a strategy and solid management. Even more than that, Apollo is a reminder of the power of the human spirit and what we can accomplish with our hearts, minds, and hard work. That can be true of virtually any project.

Now let's bring the discussion back to earth.

Start with the Big Why

The LogFrame Objectives distinguish two separate levels of *Why* the project is being done. As introduced previously, these are the Purpose and Goal.

We can think of Purpose as the near-term "Little *Why*" or "Small *Why*," and the Goal, the longer-term "Big *Why*." Calling Purpose "Little" is just a mnemonic tool to help us remember where it fits on the LogFrame (under the Big *Why*) and that it is smaller in scope (project scope rather than program scope). Once these have been established, then you can more confidently identify the project deliverables (*What*), and then the action plan (the *How*).

Perhaps surprisingly, note that during project design, Purpose takes on greater importance than the Big *Why*, as you will soon learn.

Aligning your project deliverables to these two *Whys* provides a clear direction and a focal point for execution. The trigger questions below illustrate the difference between the Goal and Purpose.

Purpose Questions	**Goal Questions**
What does the user or customer need?	Why are we doing this project?
How would the clients or users benefit from this project?	What will doing this project move us towards?
If this project were a success, how would we know?	What is the value or benefit from this investment?
What change are we intending to produce?	What is the big-picture overarching reason for this project?
What is the problem this project solves?	To what higher corporate or strategic program does this project contribute?

Some examples of Purpose statements and the corresponding Goal are below. Notice while the project by itself can achieve the stated Purpose, it is only one factor that contributes to the Goal.

Purpose	Goal
Simplify the product ⟶	Reduce customer service calls
Achieve world-wide ban on ⟶ eating small skinny dogs	Make the world safer for Chihuahuas
Increase number of firebreaks → in state forests	Reduce number of homes damaged by forest fires
Open 10 more daycare centers→ in neighborhoods	Enable more single mothers to get outside jobs
Develop a new XYZ product →	Increase company sales and profits
Increase # of qualified ⟶ leads by __%	Grow the level of high-ticket sales by __%
Learn high-impact skills ⟶	Advance my career and salary
Get in better physical shape ⟶	Look amazing for the class reunion

If you have two plausible *Why* statements and are unsure of which is Purpose and which is Goal, do the *If-Then* test. Ask it one way, then the other, and choose the sequence that makes sense.

Focus First on Purpose

A LogFrame should only have a single Purpose. That's because having only one Purpose makes it easier to identify the necessary Outcomes. Multiple Purposes dilute the project focus and muddle the design.

If you seem to have more than one valid Purpose, first check to see whether or not there is a causal relationship between your candidate Purpose statements. Often you can summarize the multiple Purposes in a single, more global statement, and capture the meaning of each aspect of the statement with Measures.

Many times, what seems like different Purposes at first glance actually mean the same thing but use different words. To discover if this is the case, ask how you would measure each one. If the Measures are the same, so too are the Objectives.

Seldom is one project sufficient to reach a significant Goal. Multiple project thrusts (each with its own Purpose) are usually needed to reach the Goal. For example, reaching the single Goal of increased profit margins may require parallel projects to reduce costs and increase sales.

Why is Purpose the most important level to focus on when designing a project? The answer is that a project is designed to *directly produce* Purpose. Having the perspective of a clear Purpose in tandem with its associated Success Measures helps to determine the set of Outcomes you need to reach that Purpose.

In addition, Purpose is more "reachable." Sometimes a Goal is broad and overwhelming, but a Purpose is within reach and is a necessary step towards that Goal. Purpose achievement should be the team's focal point—not just Outcome delivery.

Choose a Purpose verb that best captures the project intent. The most commonly used ones from Schmidt's Master Verbs Menu in Chapter 3 include these:

• Simplify	• Use	• Increase
• Improve	• Accelerate	• Revitalize
• Optimize	• Decrease	• Strengthen
• Attain	• Streamline	• Transform

Purpose should express a clear, compelling, and motivating intention agreed to by all key players.

Sharpen Your Outcomes

Outcomes are defined as the project deliverables and functioning processes needed to reach Purpose.

If there are standard steps or milestones for your type of project, you can use those to chunk (organize) your Outcomes.

But this initial clarity does not exist for discovery-type projects where learning is progressive. In its earliest stages, the Outcome set can consist of the identification and development of processes, work streams, swim lanes, and themes to explore.

Initial planning for all but the simplest projects usually requires a few iterations to arrive at an executable solution. With each planning iteration, you gain clarity. With this progressive elaboration, the problem and the solution begin to converge, and the earlier Outcomes give away to more tangible results.

Be agile in your design thinking. Start with the Purpose and identify one or two Outcomes you are sure about. As your analysis progresses, additional required Outcomes should coalesce in your mind as you zoom in on a workable solution. Allow them to evolve intelligently as you discuss, learn, and work toward the best solution.

Does your project have more than one phase, either sequential or overlapping? If so, each project phase warrants its own unique Purpose and set of Outcomes, tied to a Goal that is common across all phases. Within each phase, your choice of how to chunk the Outcomes includes chunking by:

- Major milestones
- Sequence of deliverables
- Organization entity or person responsible
- Processes or capabilities needed
- Functions that must be performed

As a rule of thumb, five to seven Outcomes (plus or minus two) are generally sufficient. You can have fewer, but if you have just one Outcome, see if it can be broken out further. If you have more, try to group them in some fashion.

Identify your MVP

You may have heard the acronym MVP used to mean a Minimum Viable Product, which is a product with a minimum set of features required to demonstrate a concept or achieve sales.

When talking about a LogFrame, we use that acronym to mean a Minimum Viable *Project*, which is a project with the minimum set of Outcomes required to achieve the Purpose.

Zappos founder Tony Hsieh began with an MVP to prove his concept. His belief (hypothesis) was *If* people saw online ads for attractive shoes, *Then* they would buy. He began his shoe business with absolutely no inventory. He would take pictures of shoes he thought would sell well online, and offer them for sale through ads.

If someone ordered a pair, he would then purchase the shoes himself and send them to the customer. It is hard to think of an easier way to determine the viability of a strategy than by doing the minimum necessary test of the concept.

The most critical LogFrame design element is the hypothesis from Outcome to Purpose, also called the *Project Design Hypothesis.* This factors in Assumptions with its *If-And-Then* construct as shown in Figure 5.5.

You should have reasonable confidence in the hypothesis: "*If* we can produce these Outcomes, *And* these Assumptions are correct, *Then* we should achieve this Purpose." Ask whether or not you have the *necessary and sufficient* set of Outcomes and Assumptions to achieve the Purpose. This is where you use the LogFrame to define, experiment with, and test your MVP. This is where you turn your hunch into a testable experiment.

As a simple example, let's say your Purpose is to be healthier and have more energy, so that you can enjoy the Goal of a long and happy life. You might start your design with Outcomes you already know about: good eating habits and an exercise routine to get you

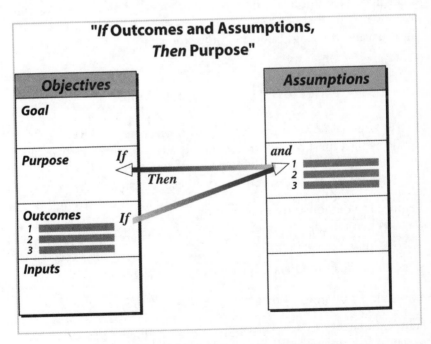

FIGURE 5.5   The Project Design Hypothesis

going. Your Assumptions may include having the support of family members with different food preferences. If you are eating well and exercising but are getting drowsy, you might expand your LogFrame to include an Outcome of getting better sleep, which may require an Assumption that your mattress is adequate to give you sufficient rest. And if that Assumption is not true, it's time for a trip to the mattress store. We will take a closer look at Assumptions in Chapter 7.

Keep It Simple

Tim McClintock is a leading strategy consultant who helps client companies scale quickly. At times he'll add actions to what they are already doing, but more often than not he recommends reducing their action items rather than adding to them.

McClintock points out what the client no longer needs to be doing and what gets in their way. He strips their actions down to the bare essence to reach their goals. Anything that does not add value towards that goal is a distraction and a complication, and increases cost and lost opportunities.

When the minimum set of necessary and sufficient actions are identified, McClintock helps his clients develop a step-by-step plan to move from their current state to where they want to be in the future, using the LogFrame and other tools.

Review These Project Designs

Let us explore how several real-world project teams developed their MVP using Question #1 to define and align their Objectives. Each example offers a starting point you can use and modify to fit your own similar projects. As you review these, consider how you might measure each Objective and what Assumptions would strengthen the *If-Then* logic.

Notice that for the Outcomes, the verbs are stated in the past tense and are usually placed at the end. This makes the expected end conditions clear and makes it easier to develop measures.

Improving a Business Process

The U.S. facility of a Japanese electronics company had three separate business units in different buildings co-located on a single site.

The three business units manufactured laptop computers, monitors, and televisions, and each had its own purchasing, inventory, and payment functions. This duplication was costly and inefficient.

During an on-site project design training workshop, participants from all three business units discussed the problem and decided to take initiative and propose a better approach. Their logic follows:

Goal:
The company better manages its financial resources.

Purpose:
Improve the purchasing/inventory/payment system.

Outcomes:
1. Solution Task Force selected.
2. Current process (as-is) documented.
3. Cause of problems clearly identified.
4. "Best practices" identified.
5. Solution parameters and system constraints defined.
6. Alternate solutions identified.
7. "To be" process designed.
8. Implementation plan developed.

The Outcome chunking here is by sequential milestones. Note that Outcome #8 is to develop an implementation plan for the next phase. It is included here as a reminder and a continuity bridge. That plan itself warrants a separate LogFrame, to be put together based on the results of the first seven Outcomes. Note that including the next phase plan as a deliverable would provide a smooth bridge to the next phase of a multiphase project.

This MVP design was sufficient to pitch to senior management who gave the go-ahead for the team to complete the plan and lead its implementation. Moreover, the team was recognized for their initiative.

Developing Internal Training Capacity

The average age of employees at this fast-growing video games company was just 27. These young enthusiastic gamers had little Project Management experience but major project responsibilities. The company needed more employees with project management skills to handle their rapid expansion. After conducting a pilot LogFrame session, they decided to create an internal capacity to train their employees in this approach and make it part of the corporate capabilities.

Vision:

Company operates smoothly, efficiently, effectively, and profitably to deliver exceptional player experience.

Goal:

Company leaders at all levels understand and are able to use LFA to plan and execute strategy initiatives of all types.

Purpose:

Company has self-sufficient internal capacity to deliver effective LFA training programs and facilitate planning sessions.

Outcomes:

1. LFA Project Team created and operating effectively.
2. Current workshop design tailored to be company-specific.
3. Additional workshops held to train participants, refine materials, and train trainer.
4. Internal trainers are coached to a certifiable level of performance.
5. Roll-out plan and schedule in place.

Note they added an additional level as Vision above the Goal, to connect to a corporate Objective, demonstrating how the LogFrame is adaptable to meet your own needs.

Growing Internal Talent

This high-tech company recognized they did not have enough "bench strength" to promote from within to fill senior-level vacancies as they arose. Their project would ensure they are building enough leadership talent to fill these positions and maintain industry leadership.

Goal:

Maintain #1 position in the X segment of the Y industry.

Purpose:

Have a deep enough talent bench to fill key positions that open up due to growth, promotion, and turnover.

Outcomes:
1. Key organization positions identified and prioritized.
2. Future skill needs projected, and gaps identified.
3. High-potential employees identified and tracked.
4. Individual development and training plans in place for all employees.
5. Succession plans developed.

One especially critical Assumption is that current employees have the ability and desire to advance.

Managing Your Professional Development

Lifelong personal and professional development is not a luxury—it is a necessity to future-proof our careers. If you consistently learn, grow, and develop new skills, you will remain competent, competitive, and able to add greater value. Your own professional development strategy should accelerate your career growth as well as improve your satisfaction. Your organization may provide some training, but the primary responsibility to develop yourself rests with you.

Goal:
Experience a challenging, satisfying career that makes a difference and provides security for my family.

Purpose:
Enhance my career capabilities, visibility, and marketability.

Outcomes:
1. New leadership and communication skills developed.
2. Knowledge of my industry/domain issues increased.
3. Comfort zone stretched by engaging in adrenalin-pumping activities.
4. Personal contact network expanded to include more "movers and shakers."
5. Online network presence increased.

Use the example above as the starting point for creating your own development strategy.

By equipping yourself with unique, value-adding, and in-demand transferable skills, you expand the possibilities available to you and buffer yourself from future career risks.

The complete LogFrames for all these examples are included in the free bonus material you can download from www.management-pro.com/bookbonus.

Review Key Points

1. Whether you aim for the moon or a target right here on our beloved planet Earth, build a strong and clear business case. Showing how your own Objectives logically connect enhances understanding of your initiative and demonstrates why your project is worthy of support.

2. Create a strong structural foundation for your project by asking and answering Question #1.

3. Recognize there are two connected levels of *Why* in the Log-Frame—Goal and Purpose—which are the Big *Why* and Little *Why*, respectively.

4. Purpose expresses the important result or impact we expect the project to produce. This is the most critical Objective to focus on during project design.

5. The Outcomes set is your solution to a problem or your way to exploit an opportunity. At first, the full set may be unclear. Start with one or two you are certain about and then add others as your planning progresses. Keep it simple.

6. Design your Minimum Viable Project by articulating the minimum set of Outcomes and Assumptions needed to reach your initial purpose.

Apply Step #1

For the best results with this and other steps, invite a few core team members to participate. You can also do this on your own, and then share the results:

1. Begin with a draft list of Objectives. Take these from a work scope or other documents if they exist; otherwise brainstorm.

Group your Objectives into those you can make happen and those you cannot. The former will become Inputs and Outcomes, while the latter will be Purpose- and Goal-level Objectives.

2. Test the logic of your Project Design Hypothesis (Outcome to Purpose linkage plus valid Assumptions). Iterate and improve.

3. Approach your projects the way a scientist would, as a carefully structured experiment. A clear set of hypotheses is the structural foundation for a successful project. Implementation results determine the validity of your hypothesis.

4. Be agile enough to modify your project design when more information becomes available and learning occurs during planning and execution.

Coming Up Next

In the next chapter we look at the second Strategic Question, "How Do We Measure Success?" You will learn how defining Success Measures adds clarity to Objectives by identifying the conditions you expect to exist in order to declare that the project is successful. And we will show how continuing to fill in pieces of the LogFrame helps to sharpen other parts of the project design, because all the cells are interrelated and interconnected.

6

Question #2—How Do We Measure Success?

You cannot manage what you cannot measure.

—Bill Hewlett, co-founder of Hewlett-Packard

Objectives	Success Measures	Verification	Assumptions
Goal			
Purpose			
Outcomes			
Inputs			

FIGURE 6.1 Success Measures Describe What Each Objective Means

Develop Success Measures and Verifications

Objectives by themselves remain vague until pinned down by valid Success Measures.

Success Measures describe the conditions expected to exist when Objectives are achieved. Clarifying these conditions early strengthens your design and reduces later disagreement over whether project Objectives have been met. At the same time that you set measures, identify the data sources needed to verify the status of each measure. Be thoughtful and selective when choosing these important guides, as they constitute items to monitor on your project dashboard.

The term *Success Measures* also goes by other names such as metrics, Key Performance Indicators (KPIs), and Key Results Areas (KRAs), among others.

This chapter includes a case study that illustrates how even the most complex Goals can be clearly measured.

Measure What Matters Most

Setting clear Success Measures at the project start does two things. First, it strengthens the project design. Second, it reduces after-the-fact doubts and finger-pointing as to whether a project reached its intended Objectives.

In the LogFrame construct, Success Measures appear in the second column (see Figure 6.1). As you would expect, for each Objective you construct a Success Measure by combining an *indicator* and its *target*. The *indicator* describes the expected type of behavior, action, or event. The *target* makes the indicators more specific by adding the required numerical value to be achieved and/or a date by when it is to be achieved. It goes without saying that measures must be *verifiable* to be useful.

One common form of measures is to "Achieve X by Y date" or "Increase X from ___ to ___ by Y date": for example, *Achieve roll-out of new product by September 1*, or *Increase customer satisfaction by 20 percent within 3 months."*

The best Measures meet these criteria:

1. *Valid*—They accurately reflect the meaning of each Objective.
2. *Targeted*—They include numerical quality, quantity, and time targets that are pinned down.
3. *Verifiable*—They can be verified by nonsubjective evidence or data.
4. *Independent*—There are separate measures at each level in the hierarchy.

Your projects may include *hard* indicators that can be easily quantified as well as *soft* indicators that are more subjective. Let's go through the various types of indicators that may apply to your project.

Hard Indicators

The following list provides examples of *hard* indicators:

- Reduce errors by 20 percent in six months
- Enhance quality by 10 percent by Q2
- Increase net profits by 15 percent this year
- Stabilize performance within one standard deviation by Y date
- Improve funding by 30 percent within six months of project start date
- Increase total # of served clients by 15 percent by the end of the year
- Relocate 50 percent of materials to X location from Y location in one month
- Reach milestone X by Y date with Z resources

These examples show a future expected completion date. You can often break these down into interim targets for ongoing progress monitoring (e.g., 20 percent by end of January, 30 percent by end of February, etc.).

In many cases, rather than locking in a single quantitative target, it makes more sense to state a range ("between X and Y"). That is especially appropriate when there is little data to justify any specific number. You can also set minimum acceptable, desired, and stretch targets. For example, increase website traffic by 10 percent minimum; 15 percent desired; and 20 percent stretch target by June 30.

A good way to begin is to simply specify the types of indicators, but leave blank placeholders for the numeric targets, unless they are readily known. With discovery-type projects, it is common to target each indicator only after further learning, analysis, or consultation.

As you proceed, remember that what is easy to measure is not always important, and what is important is not always easy to measure.

Soft Indicators

Soft indicators are those that are intangible or subject to personal judgment. They lack a clear-cut criterion for their satisfaction, but are considered to have been achieved, or *satisfied*, when there is sufficient positive and little negative evidence for its claim. But that does not mean they do not get a target date. Some examples include:

- Improve employee morale by 20 percent by end of September
- In the fall, new students to be given more help than last year
- Improve the taste of the gravy next month
- Reduce employee dissatisfaction with the leadership within three months
- Enhance employees' enjoyment of the annual summer picnic more than last year
- Ensure team communicates effectively
- Strengthen relationships among the crew
- Improve level of being candid in meetings
- Increase psychological safety on teams
- Make progress review meetings more productive

Applying the *YouTube test* can get you started in identifying soft indicators. Imagine what the video showing that the Objective has been (or is being) achieved would look like?" When you can picture the behavior or phenomenon in your mind, you can more easily choose indicators.

Targeting Your Indicators

Adding numerical values for each indicator is called *targeting*. Begin with the basic indicator, and then elaborate by describing as appropriate:

- Quantity—How many? How much?
- Quality—How good? What standards of performance?
- Time—By when? For how long?
- Customer—Who are the clients/users/beneficiaries?
- Cost—What resources are required?

Set numeric targets at a level that is sufficient to achieve the impact required at the next-higher level. Selecting appropriate targets can draw from past experience, data analysis, or negotiated agreement to establish what is realistic, achievable, and warranted. When all else fails, make a reasonable guess.

Make sure you have valid indicators that cover each key word in the statement of the Objective. Recall that the measures for Fircrest Purpose statement in Chapter 4 required five different indicators to capture each element of this multifaceted Objective.

How many Measures does each Objective need? It all depends. While a single Measure will sometimes suffice, multiple Measures are usually necessary to pin down all but the simplest Objectives. Choose the minimum number that enables you to monitor the progress toward each Objective with sufficient accuracy.

The easiest measures to monitor are at the Input and Outcomes level, which covers tasks, schedule, costs, and progress made (earned value). However, those that are the most important—those ascending towards Outcomes, Purpose, and Goal—are progressively more difficult. Purpose- and Goal-level Measures should be jointly developed and agreed upon by key stakeholders. Outcome measures are the project team's responsibility to set.

Other Variations and Combinations

The list below illustrates possible variations on the two major types described above.

- Single-point events: Complete ISO certification; Achieve break-even point

- Time period targets: Achieve X results between Jan. 1 and March 31
- Range of results: Achieve minimum level of X, a target of 1.5X, and stretch target of 2.5X
- Performance targets: Reduce errors in code to less than X
- Minimum acceptable: Reduce customer churn by at least 15 percent
- Maximum acceptable: Customer complaints not more than 2 percent
- Current Indicators: Hotel occupancy rate
- Leading Indicators: Future hotel room reservations
- Lagging Indicators: Three-month trailing average
- Proxy or substitute Indicators: Count relative plant population by pollen count
- Compound Measures: Airline revenue per passenger seat-mile

Make vague indicators clear by adding targets, as shown in Figure 6.2.

Vague	Better	Best
• Improve Sales	• Improve sales by 30%	• Improve sales of product "X" by 30% in 6 months; with half of increase coming from new customers
• Improve Teamwork	• Reduce team conflicts	• Reduce team conflicts requiring medical care by 40% next month

FIGURE 6.2   Make Measures Clear by Adding Targets

Determine How to Verify

The third LogFrame column, Means of Verification, identifies the source of data or other means to efficiently monitor and verify the status of each Measure.

Here are some examples:

- Direct observation
- Instrument reading or test results
- Decision meetings (budget approval)
- Financial reports
- Net promoter scores
- Industry financial comparisons
- Employee/Management meetings
- Industry surveys

- Completed tests
- Customer surveys
- MIS reports
- Letters of agreement
- Completed documentation
- Earned value analysis results
- Focus groups
- Industry certification
- 360-degree feedback
- Project review meetings
- Post-project evaluations

Additional verification methods include the results of any measurement or analytical tools used, such as mathematics, statistics, and computer software.

Do not rely only on reports and other system-generated information to keep your finger on the project pulse. Reach beyond databases, computers, and formal status reports, and tap into the informal network. Sometimes an informal conversation yields better insights than the most recent reports. Getting candid information requires that you create a psychologically safe environment, as discussed further in Chapter 11.

Measurement has a cost in time, energy, and resources. So, first look to already existing and easy-to-use methods, and then supplement these as needed. Sometimes getting the information you would ideally like to have is too impractical, too complex, or too expensive. Make sure the cost of identifying and monitoring does not exceed the value of the information.

The Verification column forces you to consider and concisely summarize how status information will be generated, tracked, analyzed, reported, and utilized:

- Who needs what information and why?
- What specific measures provide what is needed?

- How timely and accurate must the information be?
- What format should it be in?
- What's the best way to get and share it?

Just because you can measure something does not mean you should. Give careful thought to choosing the most appropriate measurements.

With that introduction, we will now explore how to expand and Objectives Tree and turn it into a LogFrame with clear measures and Assumption.

Measures Help You Choose Among Alternative Approaches

In Chapter 2, we introduced an Objectives Tree for customer service improvement. Recall we were comparing three different paths and the team chose to eliminate one option, leaving two third-level Objectives to evaluate further (resolve issues faster, and speed up customer learning) We pick up the story at this point.

We can expand these two remaining third-level Objectives down another level, as shown in Figure 6.3.

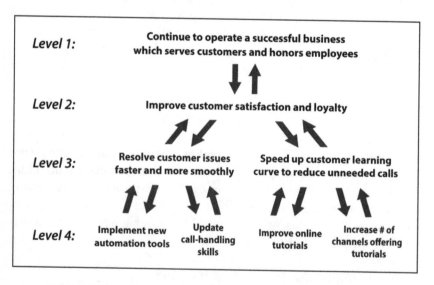

FIGURE 6.3   Objectives Tree for Improving Customer Service

This offers a better picture of how each of the two remaining third-level Objectives could be achieved. You may decide one or both are necessary to achieve our second-level Objective of improved customer satisfaction and choose to build a project around them.

We have a choice to either include both of our third-level Objectives in a single LogFrame or to divide it into two Log-Frames—one project for each third-level Objective. To keep the logic intact, if we divide it, each third-level Objective becomes an Assumption in the other's LogFrame.

For this example, we will choose to leave it all as one project and copy the Objectives to the left column of a LogFrame, shown in Figure 6.4. Then we populate the remaining cells by addressing the other Critical Strategic Questions. The resulting summary document paints a clear picture of the project strategy on a single page.

Special Types of Indicators

Two types of indicators can be particularly useful, if you know how to use them correctly: leading and proxy.

Leading Indicators

In most projects there is a lag time between Outcome completion and Purpose achievement in your project. The seeds that a farmer plants in the spring will not bring forth crops until the summer. But along the way, a smart farmer monitors leading indicators of probable success (or not) in order to adjust the plan. Soil too dry? Increase watering. Hungry birds waiting? Put up scarecrows.

Leading Indicators play an important predictive role. *If* the sales team is not meeting their weekly customer calls targets, *Then* the sales targets will not be met, nor will the financial Goal. Thus, knowing early on that targets for calling customers are not being met allows us to adjust as needed.

Have you identified leading indicators? Can you obtain early evidence that the business case is or will be fulfilled? Learn to spot trouble *before* it strikes, and decide how to prevent it! Action leads; results follow.

Objectives	Success Measures		Verification	Assumptions
Goal: Continue to operate a successful business which serves customers and honors employees	**Goal Measures:** 1. # customers increased by ____% in ____ months 2. Employee satisfaction ____% higher in ____ months 3. Sales margin not decreased over ____ months 4. Profit margins increased by ____% in ____ months		1. Monthly sales report 2. Employee survey 3. Monthly sales report 4. Monthly financial report	**To reach Goal:** 1. Marketing intelligence is correct 2. HR survey on employee needs is correct
Purpose: Improve customer satisfaction and loyalty	**Purpose Measures:** 1. Product returns reduced in first three months by ____% 2. Complaints reduced in first ____ months by ____% 3. ____% more initial customers retained after ____ months		1. RMA dept. record 2. Customer service call record 3. Monthly sales report	**To achieve Purpose:** Product quality does not decrease, price does not increase
Outcomes: 1. Resolve customer issues faster and more smoothly 2. Speed up customer learning curve to reduce unneeded calls	**Outcomes Measures:** 1.1 Number of calls transferred decreased by ____% by ____ 1.2 Number of issues resolve per call increased from ___ to ___ by ____% 2. Customer ability to complete tasks without calling increased ____% by _____		1.1 Service call record 1.2 Service call record 2. New customer sales record	**To produce Outcomes:** 1. New phone menu is clear to customers 2. % calls with multiple issues does not decrease 3. New customer sales rate does not drop
Input Tasks: 1.1 Implement new automation tools 1.2 Update call-handling skills 2.1 Improve online tutorials 2.2 Increase channels offering tutorials	**Who:**	**When:**	**Resources:**	**For Inputs:** 1. New tool within budget 2. Training is clear enough to train reps well 3. Web platform can handle all tutorials 4. Partners amenable to adding more training

FIGURE 6.4   LogFrame for Improving Customer Service

Those learning-by-doing or agile efforts that involve frequent adjustments benefit highly from leading indicators and ongoing modification in order to redirect the strategy as needed during the project journey.

Proxy Indicators

When the preferred indicators are too difficult, too expensive, or too unreliable, choose a proxy (substitute) that closely correlates with the item of interest. While proxies are never as accurate, they are often the best you can do.

The rock band Van Halen pioneered high-energy rock concerts featuring pyrotechnics and complex special effects along with their legendary music. Several huge moving vans were needed to move their massive amount of equipment from city to city. Setting up the stage correctly in each new venue according to the instructions provided was critical, but not all local crews carefully followed the steps.

So, Van Halen inserted a clause into their contract which specified that their dressing room would contain a bowl of M&Ms, with all the brown ones removed. Upon arriving at a new venue a few days ahead of the performance, they would first check the M&M bowl. If there were no brown ones, they could reasonably conclude the set-up instructions had been followed. If there were brown M&Ms in the mix, the band would double-check all the connections just to make sure the equipment had been set up properly.

What proxies might you use for hard-to-measure dimensions of your project? How will you know that people are engaged and committed? How about team effectiveness? Relations with sponsors? Stakeholder support?

Case Study: Winning the Peace After Winning the War

My appreciation of the LogFrame's power to measure complex Objectives multiplied after I served as a consultant to His Excellency the Wali (governor) of Dhofar in the Southern Region, in the Sultanate of Oman. Oman is a small Arab country tucked beneath Saudi Arabia on the edge of the Arabian Sea. While this example may be far from your field of work, it illustrates how well-chosen measures and cost-effective Verification methods enable leaders to evaluate progress towards the Goal.

In the mid-1970s, Oman was wracked by Chinese-backed insurgents from Yemen, who enticed some of the local population to rise up against the government. Following years of fighting, the war ended after the government finally found a compelling way to convince the rebels to lay down their arms and surrender: They paid them in cash.

Having won the war, His Excellency then shifted his attention to "winning the peace"—a much tougher proposition. At the time, Oman's citizens in the southern region consisted primarily of nomadic herdsmen without permanent homes. The herdsmen had to move their cattle frequently in search of scarce water, as the result of shifting rainfall patterns.

The government's strategy was to put in place a community infrastructure that would encourage stable villages to become established. His Excellency believed that by drilling deep wells and creating several dozen year-round water sources, herdsmen would settle down in permanent locations, thus building communications and contributing to stability. A plausible hypothesis.

In each community, the government would also put in place other Outcomes, such as schools, health clinics, mosques, and markets. This new physical and institutional infrastructure—when accepted and used—would produce a stable environment for social, economic, and political advancement. In brief, the logic was as follows:

Goal = Stable environment established for social, economic, and political advancement.

↑

Purpose = People accept and use infrastructure so they settle down permanently.

↑

Outcomes = Institutional infrastructure (such as wells) built in permanent village locations.

This approach had never been tried before, and there was no guarantee of success. However, without the ability to track progress using well-chosen Measures, the government would not know if the strategy was working or if the insurgency was in danger of erupting again.

Over a six-week period, I guided senior government staff in creating a master LogFrame, which was exquisitely hand-drawn by Indian draftsmen on a six-foot tall vellum document, in both English and Arabic. Between working sessions, our project team staff would travel to remote villages by helicopter, armor-plated Land Rovers, or camel to gather baseline data as well as to consult with local residents.

The complexity and multiple dimensions of the Omani Goal required a comprehensive set of Measures and Verifications, as shown in Figure 6.5. The Goal statement is adequately described using three Measures categories that cover social conditions, and a fourth that covers security. Note the specific targets under each category.

His Excellency joined us during the final session when the team briefed him about the strategy using the LogFrame. His Excellency accepted responsibility for influencing certain Assumptions beyond the team's control. The program was successful, and today Oman remains a progressive and moderate Arab nation.

The full *Win the Peace* LogFrame demonstrates how to capture a complex strategy in just three pages. This is included at *www.ManagementPro.com/bookbonus*, where you will find other LogFrame examples and additional resource material.

Select the Right Way to Verify

An unusual story from this project shows the importance of a good means of Verification. To stem the possible outbreak of a particular disease in a selected area, Omani Health Ministry officials planned to vaccinate 95 percent of the population of 6,000 in a particular area within 12 weeks. Their Means of Verification was to count the number of inoculations given, as shown Figure 6.6.

Early results were impressive. After four weeks, project data showed 4,500 people were inoculated out of a population of 6,000. In the fifth week, 5,700. At ten weeks, 9,000 people, 150 percent of the estimated population!

Wait! Something was wrong. Those in charge huddled and concluded their population estimates must have been incorrect. Only later, after interviewing villagers, did they discover the true problem.

Here is what happened. Less than 20 percent of the population had actually received an injection. But this same 20 percent returned week after week, under the false assumption if one injection is good, lots of them are even better.

The Omani program managers fell into the trap of measuring what is easy to measure (by counting the number of inoculations given,) rather than what is *important* to measure and monitor.

Objectives	Success Measures	Verification	Assumptions
Goal: Stable environment in which social and economic conditions improve throughout Southern Region/Dhofar.	**Goal Measures:** **1. Literacy rate improves:** a. Percentage of persons who can read and write at 3ʳᵈ grade level increases from ____ % in 1977 to ____ % in 1982. **2. Health standards improve:** a. Percentage of population affected by diarrhea, tuberculosis, trachoma, and other high-incidence illnesses and diseases declines from ____ % in 1977 to ____ % in 1982. **3. Security situation improves:** a. Percentage of population carrying weapons declines from ____ % in 1977 to ____ % in 1982. b. Military incidents and injuries or death resulting from armed conflict declines from ____ % in 1977 to ____ % in 1982. c. Number of enemy "adoo" who have not surrendered declines from 1977 estimate of ____ to a number which is effectively nil by 1982. **4. Economic well-being improves:** a. Average per capita income from productive work activities reaches ____ by 1982. b. Income distributed such that percentage of population at or below "marginal" level as defined by government is less than ____ % in 1982. c. ____ persons employed in livestock, agriculture and fisheries by 1982. ____ persons employed in ____ enterprises which are non-agriculture or fishing by 1982.	1. Ministry of Education figures and estimates. 2. Ministry of Public Health figures and estimates. 3. Ministry of Defense figures and estimates. 4. OHEW figures and estimates.	**Assumptions to reach Goal:** 1. Providing direct improvements in the health, education and economic status of Dhofaris will result in the support of the government, rejection of insurgent influence and national unification and stability. 2. Maintaining population in the Jebel, Negd and coastal areas and preventing mass migration to Salalah is essential. Providing direct services to those areas is a means of encouraging permanent settlements and the development of communities.

FIGURE 6.5 Goal Measure for Achieving a Stable Environment in Oman

Objectives	Success Measures	Verification
Outcomes 1. Population inoculated against disease	1. 95 % of population of 6,000 people inoculated within 12 weeks of project start	1. Count inoculations given

FIGURE 6.6 Measures and Verification for the Oman Inoculations

Had they tracked who actually received inoculation by name and village, they would have detected the problem earlier.

Fortunately, there were no serious long-term health effects to those who received multiple injections. Rest assured the managers corrected their methodology after discovering their error.

Chalk it up to inadequate education, poor means of Verification, and the lag time in analyzing collected data. The lesson: Make sure you have a valid way to verify the measures that matter most.

Review Key Points

1. Remember that what is easy to measure is not always important, and what is important is not always easy to measure. And you cannot manage what you cannot measure.

2. Success Measures consist of indicators and targets. They add clarity to Objectives by describing expected behaviors, actions, or events, including required quantitative values and dates.

3. Verifications identify the means by which Success Measures will be tracked and verified. They make you consider and concisely define how status information will be generated, tracked, analyzed, reported, and used.

4. Indicators may be quantifiable or "hard," subjective or "soft." Measures too tough or too expensive should be changed.

5. Purpose Measures describe conditions you expect when you are willing to call the project a success and should be set first. That way, you can set targets at levels that are sufficient to achieve the Purpose Measures.

6. Because Goal, Purpose, and Outcomes are independent Objectives, their Measures must be independent as well.

Apply Step #2

To move forward, you need to build on your established objectives.

1. Review the Objectives you completed in Applying Step #1. Make sure you have clear statements and valid *If-Then* logic connecting Goal, Purpose, and Outcomes.
2. Beginning with Purpose, develop clear Measures using Quality, Quantity, and Time (QQT) as appropriate (and perhaps include customer and cost). Describe each Measure with complete sentences, phrases, or bullet points. As you set Measures, choose the most cost-effective Means of Verification.
3. Make sure each Measure includes indicators and targets.
4. Set them aside for a few days, then take a fresh look. Invite input from others. Continue to improve your Measures, and do not prematurely freeze them.
5. In addition, identify a few indicators that concern the performance of your project team and management process. These process gears need to turn easily and mesh smoothly to maintain high performance.

Coming Up Next

Multiple factors outside of your control can derail your project. What can you do about these risks? This is where analysis of Assumptions enters the picture. Assumptions always exist, whether we acknowledge them or not. Many project failures arise from not identifying them well enough to mitigate the risks. Ask yourself the third Strategic Question: What other conditions must exist? And discover how they add another puzzle piece into the LogFrame solutions matrix.

7

Question #3—What Other Conditions Must Exist?

It ain't what you don't know that gets you into trouble. It's what you know for sure that just ain't so.

—Mark Twain

Objectives	Success Measures	Verification	Assumptions
Goal			
Purpose			
Outcomes			
Inputs			

FIGURE 7.1 Reduce Risk by Managing Assumptions

Surface and Test Assumptions

Every project is risky, and success is always uncertain. But too many projects falter or fail unnecessarily due to problems that could have been anticipated and mitigated during the design stage. Now we take a look at how to factor-in risk by first identifying our major Assumptions necessary to achieve our Objectives. Assumptions occupy the fourth column in the LogFrame matrix (see Figure 7.1).

We define Assumptions as factors necessary for success that may be beyond your control. Assumptions are what we believe to be true, whether based on past experiences, data, or gut feelings. Make the *implicit* assumptions floating around in your mind *explicit* by putting them in writing. Then you can examine them for probability and potential impact, and then decide how to handle.

Surfacing and testing your LogFrame assumptions is the starting point for more rigorous risk analysis. This strengthens confidence in the project hypothesis and helps you sleep at night.

Spot Trouble Before It Strikes

Mark Twain said it all. The worst Assumptions are the ones we make without being aware we are even making them or considering they might be wrong. It happens in the best of organizations.

When a well-known American electronics company first laid out a football-field sized array of television equipment in their Silicon Valley plant, intending to move them later to broadcast the Summer Olympics in Australia, they made a wrong Assumption. They initially built it using the NTSC broadcast format that is standard in North America without realizing that the PAL broadcast system is used in most of Asia and Europe. Fortunately, they fixed it in time so that everyone could watch the games. This is a good example of how the implicit assumptions we automatically make need to be verified.

Even rocket scientists can make erroneous, embarrassing, and expensive assumptions. In 1999, the Jet Propulsion Laboratory (JPL) crash-landed its Orbiter spacecraft on Mars. The JPL navigation team used the metric system of millimeters, meters and kilograms; while the spacecraft builders used the English system of inches, feet and pounds. Something was lost in translation. But since that $125 million mistake, JPL has enjoyed a string of spectacular successes.

Assumptions Operate at Different Levels

The LogFrame prompts you to think beyond the project scope boundaries and consider what else is needed to make the project work. Remember the intent of working through Assumptions is to spot potential weaknesses in advance—especially the potential deal-breaking killer Assumptions—and adjust accordingly.

Recall from Chapter 4 how Assumptions force us to expand the simple *If-Then* logic to become *If-And-Then* logic, according to our Implementation Equation™.

- *If* Inputs and valid Assumptions, *Then* Outcomes;
- *If* Outcomes and valid Assumptions, *Then* Purpose;
- *If* Purpose and valid Assumptions, *Then* Goal.

The LogFrame matrix is designed to provide a focus point for Assumptions analysis. The nature of Assumptions that link each level differ, as shown in Figure 7.2.

- **Preconditions for Inputs.** These Assumptions are the initial necessary conditions to get the project moving, such as *"Project will be approved and funded."* Capture these in the lower right-hand box of your LogFrame, and remove them when they are met.
- **Input to Outcome Assumptions.** These typically deal with sponsorship, team issues, communication, resources, dependencies, and technology. All the things you need to consider to make the project work.
- **Outcome to Purpose Assumptions.** These deal with user acceptance and the conditions that would enable acceptance and usage, along with contributing factors from other interface

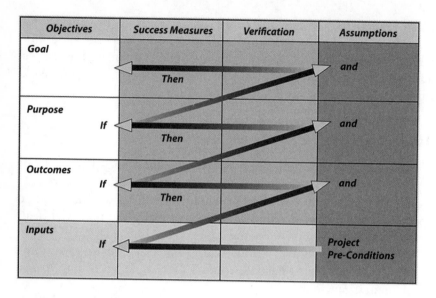

FIGURE 7.2   Different Types of Assumptions Operate at Each Level

events or projects. These are typically the weakest linkage of a project design and where, in hindsight, projects tend to fail.

- **Purpose to Goal Assumptions.** These tend to be more global and deal with the broader environment, competitors, regulations, customers, policy, and other projects that are part of the broader program strategy.

Assumptions at each level include factors beyond your ability to control, those you can influence, and those you can bring into your project, should you choose to or need to. Note that Assumptions outside your sphere of control may be within someone else's control. After all, there is no limit to what you can accomplish if you can get someone else to do the work!

Evaluate Assumptions in Three Steps

While we can never completely eliminate risks, we can reduce them to acceptable levels with the following three-step Assumptions analysis process.

Step 1—Identify Key Assumptions

Bring people with diverse perspectives and cognitive processes into the discussion. This can include advisors, selected customers, executives, and other stakeholders beyond the core team.

In each of the relevant categories below, ask What *must* we assume? And What *are* we assuming about?

- Project team members
- Stakeholders, interests
- Management support
- Technology issues
- Market and trends
- People resource availability
- Other resource availability
- Interfaces and dependencies
- Supplier and supply chain issues
- Constraints

- Cybersecurity and safety
- Customer expectations
- Team culture
- Economics and budgets
- Company political dynamics
- Potential policy or regulatory changes
- Potential impact on other projects/goals
- Competing issues

Encourage people to deliberately challenge the validity of each of the Assumption. When finished, you will have greater risk awareness and will know what to watch for.

Verify the Assumptions you can. If you were assuming Bob will be available to give half his time to this project in June, you'd better check with Bob. He did mention something about taking a long summer vacation in Yellowstone Park, which could leave boulders in your path if he plays a critical role.

Think Beyond Your Project Scope

In addition to making Assumptions about how outside factors affect your project, consider the reverse. How might your project impact other parts of the organization? If you do not consider the larger system, severe unintended consequences may occur.

Several years ago, the IT Department of a well-known candy company decided to upgrade the system used by their distributors and retailers to order products. But they chose a development time frame that overlapped with the critical months when stores ordered their Halloween candy. When the system upgrade ran into problems and ran over schedule, the ability to process orders broke down. This caused a major loss in sales and perhaps disappointed many Trick or Treaters.

Uncover Hidden Assumptions

One way to get the ball rolling is to imagine, for a moment, that it is some time in the future and the project has failed. Engage key players in considering what might have caused that failure. What Assumptions did we make that were not true? Why did it fail? What risks were we unaware of? What might we have done during initial planning to prevent this failure? Pay special attention to the potential "deal-breakers." Experience shows that many of the risks that occur at interfaces, hand-offs, phase gates, and change requests are due to communication breakdowns.

Highlight the Most Significant Assumptions

Express each Assumption as a positive condition that must exist for your *If-Then* logic to hang together. Make them specific by adding Measures because vague Assumptions hide the concern behind the issue.

Progressive elaboration leads to well-stated and clear Assumptions, as the examples in Figure 7.3 show.

Step 2—Analyze and Test Each Assumption

Having defined them, now you can test your Assumptions in order to fine-tune your approach.

Many organizations already have sophisticated risk management systems in place. If you are designing a luxury hotel to orbit the planet, you already have such a system. In other cases, the Assumptions analysis consists of more informal and subjective estimates based on experience, and it may be the best we can do. As is often the case, the Assumptions analysis will be subjective and not subject to numerical analysis.

Vague Assumptions	Better-Stated Assumptions	Best-Stated Assumptions
• Management will support the project.	• The VPs of Finance and Marketing will support the project.	• The VPs of Finance and Marketing will each allocate $100,000 from their budgets by June 30.
• Sufficient resources available.	• System analysts are available to help with the project.	• 6 senior system analysts available to help with the project in June.
• Management turnaround time acceptable.	• Prompt turnaround on deliverables submitted for approval.	• Turnaround on deliverables not more than 5 working days.
• Competitive situation stable.	• Competitor doesn't introduce similar product in the same timeframe.	• Panasonic or Apple doesn't introduce electronic gizmo with similar features at same price point in the next 8 months.

FIGURE 7.3 Expressing Well-Defined Assumptions

Chew on questions like these:

- How important is this Assumption for project success or failure?
- What is the probability this Assumption is valid (or not)?
- Can we express it as a percentage? How do we know?
- If the Assumptions fail, what is the effect on the project?
- What could cause this Assumption to *not* be valid?"

At this point in your Assumptions analysis you are likely to assess risks as HIGH, MEDIUM, or LOW according to their impact on one or more of your project's key success criteria. For HIGH and MEDIUM you need a risk-reduction plan. You can put LOW risks on a watch list. The conventional ways to handle risk are through avoidance, transference, mitigation, sharing, and acceptance.

You can also construct a simple Probability and Impact (P&I) matrix to rate each risk and estimate the likelihood of occurrence.

Even when done informally, the Assumptions discussion will reveal easily overlooked issues that deserve to be on your radar.

Step 3—Act on Them

Now comes the critical part. Put each key Assumption under your mental microscope and consider the following:

- Is this a reasonable risk to take?
- To what extent is it amenable to control?
- Can we manage it? Influence and nudge it? Or only monitor it?
- Is this Assumption under someone else's control?
- What remediation or contingency plans might be put in place just in case?
- How can we adjust the project design to minimize the impact of, or work around, questionable Assumptions?

Though Assumptions have been defined as factors beyond your control, this is not always true. Some positive actions you can take follow.

- **Take Control.** There are times when you must bring an Assumption into your project to and make it happen because it is critical, and the project would not otherwise happen. But this takes more resources and expands the scope. Do it if only you must.
- **Give Control.** Alternatively, you can make sure it is an Objective in someone else's project. As your project progresses, collaborate on status of the item.
- **Influence or Nudge.** Though beyond your direct control, you can sometimes influence conditions underlying the Assumption in the right directions. Example Assumption: *We maintain support from senior management.* You can influence this by providing regular briefings.
- **Monitor and Respond.** When the issues are way outside your zone of control, the best you can do is keep an eye on them—continually if necessary. Scan your organizational and external networks and information sources broadly. Be alert to signals and conversations that matter. (Interest rates, competitor

moves, and the cost of commodities.) Take positive action where you can.

- **Change the Project Design.** Add Outcomes or Input tasks to work around those pesky issues or create a related project that will avoid any troubling Assumptions.
- **Prepare Backup Plans.** For example, if it absolutely, positively must get there overnight, send identical packages by DHL, UPS, and FedEx. If storms are brewing, nail on plywood and get a gasoline-powered pump before the hurricane hits! You get the idea.
- **Do Nothing.** Continue as is and accept the risk. Your reasoned judgment says it is unlikely to have a large impact, and the resources are not available (or at a reasonable cost) to manage it anyway.

Remember as your project evolves, new Assumptions will come into play as new circumstances evolve. Periodically refresh your Assumptions list and update any risk registers.

Keep the Assumptions Meaningful

When you move from analysis to documentation, decide which Assumptions to highlight in the LogFrame. Do not list the highly certain Assumptions or the very unlikely ones (i.e., "A miracle of some sort will happen"). Instead, document those you need people to keep an eye on.

The following case study brings together many of the concepts covered so far, including Objectives Trees, phase chunking, and Log-Frames. This project required an extensive analysis of many types of Assumptions.

Case Study: Battling the Asian Gypsy Moth Invasion

My phone rang. It was Jim, a recent attendee at my project planning workshop. I could hear the desperation in his voice.

"They have invaded and threaten enormous destruction. They must be killed. Time is short. Please help."

"Whoa, Jim, who invaded?"

"It's my worst nightmare."

"Jim, who invaded?"

"The Moths!"

While I could not imagine moths harming more than a wool sweater, he was alarmed. Jim was the chief moth expert at the Washington State Department of Agriculture (WSDA).

"This is not just any moth. It's the dreaded *Asian gypsy moth*. They are the King Kongs of the moth world, and now threaten to wipe out forests of the Pacific Northwest. They enter as larvae aboard ships from Siberia, grow into moths, lay more eggs, and rapidly spread. They eat everything in their path, even our evergreen trees, leaving just brown trunks and twigs."

"It's getting warm, and they will soon hatch and spread like wildfire. The U.S. Forest Service will put a dozen helicopters in the air and spray over 40,000 acres to kill them. My team's job is to find and kill those they miss. We use cardboard traps with a sticky chemical that attracts them. They get stuck and die."

Jim continued, "We face huge challenges. Within eight weeks, we need to grow from six people to almost 300, hire and train trappers, set up monitoring systems, and import and deploy tens of thousands of traps across nine counties. Also, educate the public, so they do not panic when helicopters spray their neighborhoods. And do all this out of a slow government bureaucracy."

"Jim, why do this, what's the goal?"

"To save our forests from destruction. If we fail, the economic devastation has been estimated at 54 billion dollars."

Wow! This was a serious problem with technical, organizational, and political dimensions. This project needed to start fast and keep moving fast to succeed. The short time fuse and high cost of failure left little margin for error.

"Okay, count me in."

The next morning, we met with his core team at a Starbucks near the state capital. As Jim explained the project, I sketched an Objectives Tree on a napkin to help us envision the big picture and the context for our plans, as illustrated in Figure 7.4.

The Objectives in the center column (black arrows) were the WSDA's responsibility. Other organizations were responsible for the

Objectives Tree for Combating the Asian Gypsy Moth Invasion

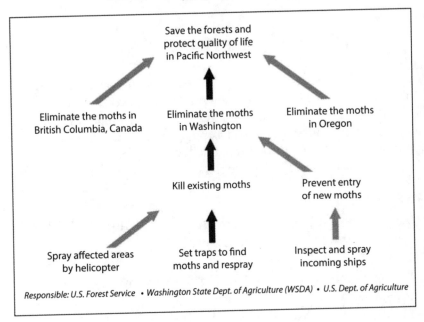

FIGURE 7.4   Asian Gypsy Moth Objectives Tree

Objectives in the two outer columns (gray arrows). These became Assumptions from WSDA's perspective.

Reading up from the bottom summarized how setting traps would ripple up the chain in *If-Then* fashion, leading to save the forests, and protect the quality of life in the Pacific Northwest. We chunked the project into four sequential phases:

- **Mobilization.** Set up monitor systems, hire and train people, set out traps.
- **Operations.** Ensure trappers check traps, record information, and send caught moths to headquarters for analysis.
- **Demobilization.** Collect and recycle all the traps at summer's end.
- **Evaluation.** Analyze project data to determine project effectiveness and lessons learned.

Separate LogFrames were developed for each phase. Each one shared the same Goal but had separate Purposes and Outcomes.

Turn Objectives Trees into LogFrame Plans

Working from their Objectives Tree, we began constructing their Mobilization LogFrame, adding the phrase to "protect the economy" as the top-level Objective and calling it a "Super Goal" to highlight the program's importance. This also keeps the logical links intact by "pinning" deliverables at the Outcome level.

Their Mobilization phase logic was:

Super Goal:

Save the forests; protect the high quality of life in the Pacific Northwest.

Goal:

Eliminate the Asian Gypsy Moth in Washington State.

Purpose:

Find and kill moths remaining after spraying.

The chunking logic chosen for the Outcomes was along organizational lines. They summarized the major Outcome that each of the five relevant organization units were responsible for. In addition, they added Evaluation as a sixth Outcome, aimed at continuous learning and improvement.

Their mobilization LogFrame appears in Figure 7.5 (inputs not included).

Examine Critical Assumptions

Murphy and his infamous law hide in the Assumptions Column, just as moths hide in the forest. This was an Assumption-driven project. Success depended on wide range of valid Assumptions covering environmental factors, politics, organization issues, scientific factors, and more. Some of these are listed below, along with the issues or actions they triggered as they evaluated each.

No unknown introductions from unexpected sources. They sprayed thousands of acres where moths were spotted. They believed moths came early from Siberian ships only, but they would be alert for other possible sources. This was a risk to accept and watch for.

U.S. Department of Agriculture (USDA) program successful in excluding entry of new moths through ports. This was beyond their control, but unless the ships were thoroughly disinfected, this might be a problem. To mitigate the risk, Jim's team developed and shared protocols on ways to properly disinfect.

Science Advisory Panel recommendations are accurate. The National Science Foundation recommendation of 16 traps per acre were considered valid, given the reputation of the scientists involved.

There are no moth infestations in areas outside the spray zone. Could there be infestations outside the spray zone? Certainly. What's the likelihood? This would require a guess. They could reduce risk by widening the spray zone to create a buffer, but at increased cost.

Pass environmental assessments. If they did not pass, their project would halt. Out of their control, but perhaps not out of their influence.

Governor declares state of emergency during the week. This was an interface with another organization. Draft a statement for the governor and arrange press conference.

Project team able to motivate trappers, low turnover. Inspecting up to a thousand traps weekly was boring work. So, they scheduled Friday night events for trappers to share what they'd learned, celebrate, and give recognition. Their BEAT THE MOTH logo pin created a sense of commitment and reaffirmed everyone's role in saving the forests, and protecting the economy and way of life.

How did this project turn out? The evaluation in phase 4 showed very few moths were caught, which indicated success of the spraying. The learning point to emphasize here is how the Assumption analysis identified additional necessary tasks they might have missed had they skipped this analysis. The same holds true for yours.

Logical Framework for
Combating the Asian Gypsy Moth Invasion

Objectives Logical hierarchy of If-Then Objectives	Success Measures Conditions when Objectives are achieved	Verification Source of evidence to verify Measures	Assumptions Additional factors necessary for success
Super-Goal: 1. Save the forests, protect the economy, and the quality of life in the Pacific Northwest.	**Super-Goal Measures:** 1. Environmental and economic damage from AGM is negligible.	1. WSDA records	**Assumptions to reach Super-Goal:** 1. No unknown introductions from unexpected sources. 2. Similar programs in Canada and Oregon are effective.
Goal: Eliminate the Asian Gypsy Moth in Washington State.	**Goal Measures:** 1. By June, AGM is under control in Washington State. No further egg masses or live moths found. 2. Systems in place in ports of entry to prevent new moths, larvae, or egg masses from entering the state.	1. WSDA records 2. Evaluation, spot checks of ships.	**Assumptions to achieve Goal:** 1. USDA program successful in excluding entry of new moths through ports. 2. Government agencies will cooperate and work together well. 3. Adequate funding with both public and political support game(s).
Purpose: Find and kill moths which remain after spraying.	**Purpose Measures:** 1. From May–September, WSDA set up and operate a survey and trapping system over target zone of 19 counties (10, 725 square miles). 2. Field team of 51 supervisors and 219 trappers work efficiently to set 180,000 traps, inspect them regularly, and send all caught moths to WSDA for identification and analysis.	1. Project evaluation 2. Project records, trap data sheets, WSDA reports.	**Assumptions to achieve Purpose:** 1. Project team will manage well. 2. Science Advisory Panel recommendations are accurate (e.g., concerning trap density). 3. There are no moth infestations in areas outside the spray zone.

If → Then

If → Then

Logical Framework for
Combating the Asian Gypsy Moth Invasion

If ↻ Then

Objectives	Success Measures	Verification	Assumptions
Logical hierarchy of If-Then Objectives	Conditions when Objectives are achieved	Source of evidence to verify Measures	Additional factors necessary for success
Outcomes:	**Description of Successful Outcomes:**	**Verification:**	**Assumptions to Produce Outcomes:**
1. Plans developed and systems put into place to rapidly launch the project and manage it successfully. (Incident Commander)	1.1 During Project Week 1, core team does rapid planning to clarify objectives, agree on roles, identify Assumptions, and create schedules.	1.1 Completed master schedule and other project documents.	1. AGM team can smoothly grow from 3-person staff in mid-February to 280-person staff by mid-May.
	1.2 Plans updated on regular basis throughout project.	1.2 Updated plans	2. Environmental assessments (3/15) will have a FONSI (Finding of No Significant Impact) and program can proceed.
2. Public understanding and support obtained. (Public Information Officer)	2.1 Through multiple channels, public meetings & 800#, public informed and support obtained.	2.1 Phone records	3. Adequate supply of traps; pheromone (moth sex lure) can be imported from Europe in time.
	2.2 Legislative briefings, public meetings, and press conferences held Week 3.	2.2 Briefing notes	4. Government administrative systems can respond fast enough to hire people on an accelerated basis.
3. Field staff recruited and hired. (Personnel Director)	3.1 Recruitment plans developed by Week 2 to hire 7 regional supervisors & 45 field supervisors before first cycle of hiring/training/deploying Week 10.	3.1 Payroll records	5. Governor Booth Gardner will declare state of emergency during week 4.
4. Field teams deployed, trained, and operate effectively as they set and inspect traps, and send all caught moths for analysis. (Operations)	4.1 Beginning Week 10, there are 4 cycles of hiring and training field sups, who then hire, orient, and deploy a total of 219 trappers.	4.1 Review of operations	6. There is a pool of 220 potential trappers available during time period and willing to work for $6.25 per hour.
	4.2 All 180,000 traps set by mid-July; quality control system operating to inspect all traps weekly and send all catches to WSDA for identification.	4.2 Trap data sheets, Quality Control System records.	7. Other government agencies project team able to motivate trappers; low turnover.
5. Supplies and equipment necessary to support trapping operations identified procured. (Logistics Chief)	5.1 All supervisors and trappers supplied with needed supplies and equipment. Each field team member is issued a vehicle and radios as needed.	5.1 Inventory checklists	8. Quality control system is effective in finding moths; any problems swiftly identified and corrected.
6. Project evaluated and improved. (All)	6.1 Ongoing operations reviewed periodically during project & improvements identified & implemented.	6.1 Weekly AGM project team meetings and decisions.	
	6.2 At end of project, entire operation reviewed, along with analysis of catch records.	6.2 Evaluation plan and USDA records.	

FIGURE 7.5 Logical Framework for Combating the Asian Gypsy Moth Invasion

Review Key Points

1. Many project disappointments spring from faulty, ill-formed, undefined, or unexamined Assumptions that could have been anticipated. Assumptions always exist, whether or not we acknowledge or verify them. Make your implicit Assumptions explicit. Get them out of your head and onto paper.

2. Because Assumptions are often the most critical factor in project success, take time to identify, examine, and validate the critical ones upon which your strategy rests.

3. Use a simple analysis matrix to evaluate them. Look for deal-breaking, project-killing Assumptions early, and address them.

4. To be most useful, formulate Assumptions as the desired conditions. Include Measures as appropriate and place them at logical project levels.

5. Determine if any of your Assumptions are the part of another team's project. Communicate with them in order to minimize the negative impact their plans could have on your project (and vice versa).

6. You have multiple options for dealing with Assumptions. You can take control, give control, influence or nudge, monitor and respond, change the project design, prepare back-up plans, add tasks, or do nothing.

Apply Step #3

Squeeze out known and knowable project bugs by examining your Assumptions using this process:

1. Identify all key Assumptions in your project, especially the mission-critical (a.k.a. "killer") ones.

2. Analyze their probability and the consequences of their impact, along with the various means and costs of possible deflection or amelioration by your team.

3. Act to manage what you can. Before faulty Assumptions cause trouble, beef up defenses to prepare for their arrival, and communicate effectively with other stakeholders as warranted.
4. Set up a risk register and a way to track emerging signs of something going awry, particularly for high-severity events.

Coming Up Next

Now we are ready to develop the execution plan. If Outcomes are well defined, we use one form of project planning to reach your Goal. But what do we do if Outcomes are not well defined, or are expected to evolve as the project matures? The next chapter discusses the fourth Strategic Question, that now considers how to plan to execute the project. And we will see how the LogFrame strategy supports a variety of project lifecycles as a high-level strategic summary rather than a detailed action plan.

8

Question #4—How Do We Get There?

Let our advance worrying become advance thinking and planning.

—Winston Churchill

Objectives	Success Measures	Verification	Assumptions
Goal			
Purpose			
Outcomes			
Inputs			

FIGURE 8.1 Inputs Summarize the Implementation Plan

Identify Action Steps

By thoughtfully answering the first three questions, you can now lay out the implementation plan with greater certainty. Here you may bring in other management tools needed to guide implementation, depending on the type of project and the lifecycle model it follows (see Figure 8.1).

The LogFrame supports a wide variety of project lifecycles, from highly predictive waterfall plans to highly adaptive discovery-type plans, to hybrids of several. Regardless of the project type or lifecycle, most projects need to adapt as challenges arise, and follow some form of action learning cycle.

Build It Big

My introduction to project management was literally a pain in the rear. This happened in college when I built—*by hand*—what must have been the world's biggest bar chart (or Gantt chart). This project deserves a footnote in Project Management History, if not a mention in *The Guinness Book of World Records*.

As an aerospace engineering sophomore at the University of Washington in Seattle, I took a part-time job with Boeing advertised as a "hands-on project management role" to set up the project-tracking system to roll out the very first Boeing 747. This was before project scheduling software was available. At the time, it sounded exciting!

The true meaning of "hands-on" became clear on my first day when I was handed a box of quarter-inch thick black tape and instructed to affix parallel grid lines on a mile-long white Formica wall in a tunnel under Boeing's manufacturing facility. I'm not exaggerating when I say it was a mile long. Boeing's plant in Everett, Washington, is one of the world's largest buildings—you can even fit all of Disneyland inside the building!

The top parallel line had to be seven feet high. I stood on my tip-toes to spread my roll of tape. Then, I'd drop down eight inches and tape another mile-long strip. The bottom few rows required I crawl; and for the very bottom row I sat and scooted my sore and aching rump down the cold concrete floor. You can imagine how long it might have felt to tape one entire mile-long wall scooting on my fanny. So far, I did not love "hands on project management." They may have called it "hands on," but I had another more anatomically accurate phrase in mind.

After the horizontal lines were complete (and my bottom badly bruised) it was time to paste in the vertical grid lines, one for each day counting down to aircraft roll-out. This meant stretching on my tiptoes to reach the top and bending down to my toes at the bottom. Now I had an aching back to join my aching butt. When I finished, the Boeing engineers populated cells of my jumbo grid with blocks of text, identifying tasks on the critical path to get this ground-breaking aircraft into the air. Today, a simple software program could handle this task quite easily.

Working in that tunnel for what seemed to be endless, long, and boring days was disheartening. Until one magnificent day, when a production supervisor walked me around the plant for a close-up look at the very first 747. I could literally touch this wondrous piece of technology coming together on the assembly line. The concentric ribbing of the partially finished fuselage looked like the skeleton of a colossal soaring pterodactyl ready to take flight through the giant building!

When the production supervisor explained how this airplane would revolutionize travel, it was like a light bulb coming on in my head. For the first time, I understood how my work connected to the bigger picture. My thoughts went something like the following:

- *If* I build this giant grid, *Then* engineers can track the project.
- *If* they track the project, *Then* they can launch the first 747.
- *If* they launch the 747, *Then* people can fly farther and cheaper to see the world.
- *If* people can fly farther and cheaper to see the world, *Then* people can design their dream lives.

Now I understood how my Godzilla-sized grid fit into the grander scheme of things. Knowing that my work truly mattered gave me a deep sense of purpose. I felt like the janitor President

Kennedy met in 1962 when he toured a NASA facility for the first time. When the President casually asked what he was doing, the janitor replied, "I am helping put a man on the moon!"

I was no longer mindlessly taping a mile-long wall, I was launching the first-ever 747 and making worldwide travel possible! Even though my job seemed insignificant, seeing how my role connected to the higher Vision motivated me to lay down those black lines with precision and pride.

You can create that sense of connection to something important in every project. That ability to touch heart and head makes you an inspiring project leader.

Gateway to Multiple Execution Tools

Question #1 through Question #3 enable the LogFrame to function as a high-level project design. Adding Question #4 enables it to also function as an implementation planning tool. By visualizing the larger context of Objectives, Measures, and Assumptions, you can now develop action plans with more confidence.

The LogFrame structure is a jumping-off point for choosing the execution planning and tracking tools your project requires.

Your choice of methodology and tools depends on the nature of your project, with the degree of uncertainty being a key factor. Projects with low uncertainty are called *predictive* projects, while those with high uncertainty are called *adaptive*. Most projects have elements of both.

Figure 8.2 illustrates a small sample of common tools used for predictive projects. Others include affinity diagrams, control charts, flowcharts, histograms, matrix diagrams, mind maps, scatter diagrams, checklists, issue lists, logs, and many more.

For Agile and other adaptive projects, add burn-down charts, backlogs, sprints, user stories, epics, daily stand-ups, Scrum, and Kanban. Rather than go into detail on any of them here, refer to the *Fast Forward MBA in Project Management* by Eric Verzuh. Verzuh's book is a comprehensive and brilliant international best-seller, which is used in more MBA and PM programs than any other text.

With that perspective, let us explore the types of project lifecycles.

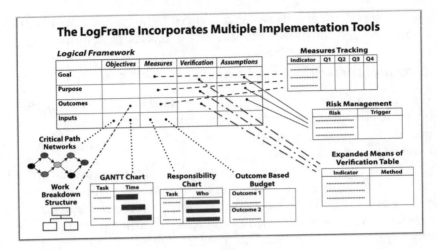

FIGURE 8.2 Common Monitoring Tools for Predictive Projects

Decide Which Lifecycle Fits Best

The following five project lifecycle types are not either–or choices; the best choice is often a combination. Regardless of the type, the LogFrame works well as the front-end planning tool for any of them.

1. Predictive Lifecycle

The predictive lifecycle is driven by known, fixed requirements; and implementation follows a predictable sequence and critical path. This lifecycle is common in construction or product development, where the three major constraints (scope, schedule, and cost) are defined in the initial phases of the lifecycle. These projects consist of multiple phases, which can either be sequential or overlapping, building upon one another to achieve the end result.

You can plan the entire project at a high level from the beginning, and then follow as a rolling-wave planning approach. This is where you complete a high-level plan for the entire project, with detailed planning done only for work that needs to be accomplished in the immediate future. With predictive projects, the initial set of Outcomes is not likely to require major change. The level of uncertainty is low because best practices and processes often exist from prior experience.

Projects with greater uncertainty need to be more adaptive (flexible) and follow one of the more adaptive lifecycles, described below.

2. Iterative Lifecycle

When you first dive into a new project, you may not know the probable solution, or even the extent of the problem. For these higher-risk projects where you do not fully know the scope at the beginning, an iterative lifecycle is a must.

With an iterative approach, changes in direction are incorporated at regular intervals through multiple cycles of planning, action, and assessment. The scope evolves as the project progresses. Each iteration reveals new information and lessons learned that impact the requirements. There is one final product delivery at the end of the last iteration.

The Apollo program followed an iterative approach, with Apollo Flights 1–10 all building on each other to provide the learning needed to make Apollo 11 and subsequent moon landings successful.

Innovation in general follows this iterative process. In fact, it is how Edison created the light bulb, by conducting thousands of experiments until he found the right filament. He had a clear goal, which was to create light from electricity. But at the start, he did not know what the solution would be or the path to get there. So, he tested, failed, and learned until finally he found the solution.

While this cycle can apply to building a physical product, it is especially appropriate for all types of *knowledge work*, such as research, organizational improvement efforts, and change projects of all types. The Outcome set can consist of processes, work streams, swim lanes, and thematic areas, rather than fixed deliverables.

3. Incremental Project Lifecycle

Incremental approaches share some of the same characteristics as the iterative because they both involve dynamic requirements and multiple cycles of work periods.

However, while the iterative approach seeks to improve what was already completed with each new iteration, the incremental lifecycle instead makes progress in small increments with the scope of work being built out over time. Activities are designed to be performed only one time for each increment, and each new increment adds additional functionality.

Take, for example, developing a fully functional website. New functionality is being added to the website with each iteration, while the full website is delivered to the customer at the end of the project.

Writing this book followed this approach as well, with multiple revisions of each chapter to polish it up until a quality manuscript was completed and submitted to the publisher.

4. Adaptive (Agile) Lifecycle

The Agile method is increasing in popularity and finding application far beyond the software industry, where it was born. With the Agile approach, teams accomplish their planning in brief iterations with short feedback loops and frequent incremental adjustments.

The Agile process involves identifying and testing short-term, smaller-scale hypotheses. Agile's key attraction is its ability to be highly adaptive, so that you can learn as you go. This works well when there can be no detailed plan on how to get from beginning to end. The philosophy behind Agile is useful for any project with dynamic characteristics, which will, by their very nature, involve continuous discovery, learning, and clarification as you proceed on the project journey.

Agile employs a combination of both iterative and incremental, but with shorter iterative sprints, typically two to four weeks in duration.

For example, if you were developing a smart phone app for iOS or Android, you might divide the project into eight sequential sprints or iterations. Each sprint culminates in a *release* (delivery of a working product) you can show to the customer.

Agile is well-suited for projects where the scope is difficult to define upfront and may be expected to change rapidly. The work, along with the frequent changes to scope, is handled in short, rapid sprints. These sprints can happen sequentially or overlap, depending on need. Risk is minimized due to the short sprint durations and frequent changes.

Short, daily meetings among team members—known as the stand-up, the morning roll call, or daily scrum—keep the plan alive.

5. Hybrid Lifecycle

Some combination of these various approaches usually ends up being the best choice.

The hybrid approach is *predictive* for those areas where work is clearly understood and well-defined, and is *adaptive* for those parts of the project where the scope is not well understood or well-defined in advance. Identify your key outcomes or work streams, and then integrate them into an overall approach.

Your chosen approach and processes need to mesh with related systems, organization culture, and nature of the business.

Discover what works best by innovating along the way. Remember Steve Jobs' advice regarding simplicity. Do not overcomplicate things. Make your system fit the context. Evolve. Adapt. Simplify.

It is worth reinforcing here how the LogFrame supports any and all of these lifecycles as an up-front design process. Always refer back to the top three rows of the LogFrame, especially when you may find yourself adding features or functionality that adds unnecessary complexity with little or no value.

Fighting Scope Creep

During project execution, the LogFrame also serves as a significant anchoring reference point. It helps to simplify and avoid scope creep (additional tasks that creep in and enlarge the scope or size of the project). Unless someone can demonstrate how adding more tasks can directly impact the Outcomes and Purpose, they cannot be justified. It also reminds the team not to be distracted and waste effort on activities that do not propel them forward.

Manage the Ongoing Strategic Action Cycle

All projects move forward in structured cycles of review and refinement in some fashion. The well-known Shewhart PDCA Cycle (Plan, Do, Check, Act) commonly used in industry is one example. Let us build a more inclusive model of project cycles that begins with a strategy/program focus.

The four elements of Strategic Action Cycle are Think–Plan–Act–Assess, as shown in Figure 8.3.

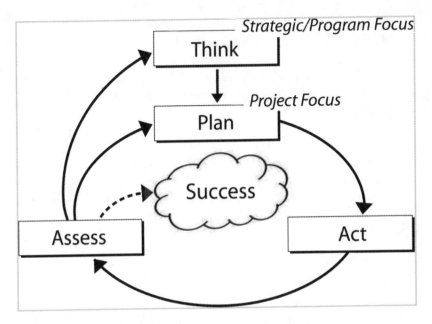

FIGURE 8.3 Strategic Action Cycle

Think is the big-picture strategic/program perspective, where Goals are defined and priority projects are identified. This function may be performed by senior leaders with results handed off to others to implement. Approved projects then drop from the Think box into the Plan–Act–Assess loop where project teams pick up the ball.

Plan the projects with the LogFrame as a continual reference, ensuring that the project design logically connects to the Goals.

Take Action and implement according to your plan but stay nimble.

Assess by periodically stepping back from the immediate day-to-day to evaluate progress and redirect as needed. Assessment is where to decide if a pivot to a new direction is needed.

Pivoting means changing course. Watch Michael Jordan or LeBron James or any basketball great pivot. If they encounter obstacles on their path to the basket, they temporarily stop, quickly assess their options, and act accordingly by passing to an open man or taking a shot. The Assess block completes the loop in three possible ways as discussed below.

The three types of Assessment—*Monitor, Review,* and *Evaluate*—should be built into every project plan. These three types differ in frequency and purpose.

Every project navigates this cycle many times and with varied frequency. Some project components have their own cadence and rhythm.

Think of the cycle in Figure 8.3 as a clock with three hands all geared together, which circle at different speeds. *The second-hand* circles most quickly as teams have daily meetings or scrums (monitor). *The minute hand* progresses with each two-to-four-week sprint (review). *The hour hand* advances more slowly through each of the project phases (evaluate).

Keep Your Project on Track

You can ensure that your project proceeds well by actively putting the three types of assessment into practice.

Assessment Practice #1: Monitor

Monitoring is the ongoing ground-level tracking of progress towards Outcome delivery. This involves using real collected data and can occur as frequently as daily, as in Agile stand-up meetings.

The dynamics of most projects require multiple means of monitoring to assemble a viable and useful picture of what is happening. Examples of real-time data sources are:

- Actively communicating with task managers
- Reviewing messages and reports
- Monitoring real-time or near-time data that relates to the key Success Measures
- Touching base with key stakeholders
- Monitoring the status of deliverables
- Checking indicators on project dashboards and other tracking tools

Assessment Practice #2: Review

While monitoring asks, "Are we on track?" review asks, "Are we on the *right* track?" The more volatile your environment or exploratory your project, the more frequently reviews should occur.

Review means stepping back from day-to-day work to reassess your approach. It challenges and invites changes to the project design, in particular the Outcome to Purpose hypothesis. Reviews should occur at milestone completion, major decision points, and transitions into the next phase of an initiative. For multi-phase projects, the formal review at the end of each phase enables making smart "go/no-go" decisions about whether to proceed and how.

Below are some Project Reviews questions:

- What progress have we made? (earned value)
- What issues have come up?
- How has our understanding of the problem changed? The solution approach?
- Is the project still relevant?
- What is the status of budget and schedule?
- How are stakeholder relationships?
- Are we likely to achieve our Purpose with this plan? Is there a better way?
- What actions do we need to take now?

Reviews typically result in updating plans and continuing the cycle. Reviews may conclude that project success has been achieved as defined by Purpose, even without completion of all the Outcomes. Bingo! Should these reviews conclude the project is no longer viable, a strategy "Rethink" is warranted.

Reviews are not the time to play the blame game if things are off track. Assume best intentions on the part of others, even if they messed up. Be hard on the problem and easy on the people.

Refresh the plans after each review. Update your LogFrame to document the evolution of major design changes. You can give it a revision number and date, making it a control document that can be integrated into the formal system.

Assessment Practice #3: Evaluate

Evaluate after the project is complete. Review evidence of Purpose- and Goal-level achievement, and other expectations as outlined in the business case or project justification.

- What went right, and why? What went wrong, and why?
- What evidence is there the project made a difference?
- Was it worth the investment of time and money?
- Were we to do this over again, what would we do differently?
- How well did we manage implementation?
- How successful was our overall strategy?
- What did we learn that was worth learning?

Make sure to identify, document, and incorporate actionable lessons learned for future use.

After the project is complete, there will be plenty of reasons from team members to avoid the evaluation step: they are too weary, too drained, too busy, reassigned, promoted, demoted, moving on. Guard against this by building *Evaluate* milestones into the project plan, so expectations are clear from the beginning.

Review Key Points

1. The LogFrame is a project front-end design tool that can be used in every type of project lifecycle. Make your LogFrame a high-level summary rather than a detailed action plan.

2. The LogFrame structure affords great flexibility and syncs up with any project phase and pace. Once Outcomes are clear, the Inputs can be illustrative, rather than definitive. They are simply the starting points for more detailed planning using other task management tools.

3. Keep your project moving forward by following the Strategy Action Cycle with an ongoing cycle of Think, Plan, Act, and Assess. Each aspect has its own frequency and cadence.

4. You do not have to use the same execution approach for all parts of your project. Use what works best for various parts of the project. Hybrids are usually the wisest choice.

Apply Step #4

Now you just need to determine how to best move forward for your Outcomes.

1. Select the project lifecycle logic that best fits your project.
2. For a simple predictive project, confirm the Outcomes as the necessary and sufficient set needed to reach the Purpose. Then list key activities for each Outcome, not more than five to seven per Outcome, so you do not get overwhelmed. Identify task sequences with a Gantt chart or network diagram, and identify resources needed for each task.
3. For adaptive projects, break the requirements into chunks, prioritize these in a list of deliverables, decide how many iterations will be needed, and stay open to continual changes as the project scope and solution approach evolve over time and become more and more well-defined.

Coming Up Next

Now that we have done a deep dive into the technical aspects of LogFrame and the four Strategic Questions, in Part III you will learn how to put it into practice and get a smooth start up. We also cover managing your "inner game", working with your stakeholders, building the foundation for a smooth and friction-free start, and using the LogFrame process to manage your life and career. You will also see a simple strategy refresh process to apply at the team, group, department, or organization-wide level.

Part III

Putting These Concepts into Practice

Prior chapters guided you in designing a project by plugging the answers to the Four Critical Strategic Questions into the LogFrame structure. Part III covers other essential elements for getting the results you seek.

- *Chapter 9* details how to get a fast and smooth start on your project.
- *Chapter 10* explores how to leverage your mindset in order to amplify your effectiveness.
- *Chapter 11* examines ways to manage team dynamics through clarity, caring, and communication.
- *Chapter 12* invites you to put these concepts into action in your own life.

9

Getting Your Project Off the Ground

Let our advance worrying become advance thinking and planning.

—Winston Churchill

If you read this book with a specific project in mind and are eager to get started, this chapter lays the groundwork to move your project into action.

One of the most important first steps is to examine the project from a strategic, business, technological, cultural, and political perspective. This understanding will serve you well.

Now is the time to begin putting your core team together, developing relationships with key stakeholders, socializing your project ideas, and preparing for two key meetings: a project design workshop where the LogFrame will be assembled, and a project kick-off meeting at which it is presented.

You will find a case study on how to refresh or pivot your strategy. This method applies to all strategic planning, strategy refinement, and organization improvement initiatives.

Move from Storming to Performing

We all want to launch our projects rapidly and gain high momentum early. But we also know successful fast launches are rare. What is it that causes launch failures, and what can we do to avoid it? To understand this phenomenon, we turn to psychologist Bruce Tuckman's classic model of team development, shown in Figure 9.1.

Tuckman identified five development stages that teams go through to deliver results. He labeled these stages Forming, Storming, Norming, Performing, and Adjourning.

In the **Forming** stage, there is uncertainty and high dependence on the project leader for guidance. Roles and responsibilities have not yet been established clearly, and the leader is likely fielding questions about the project scope. During this initial stage, the project leader acts as a *director*.

The **Storming** stage occurs after the project team is formed, and this is where projects most often falter. During this stage, people jockey for position or try to usurp the leader's authority. Some will question the worth of the project; others may resist their roles. Diverse working styles can collide and frustrate. We want teams to storm, but to do so in a healthy way. Here is where the project leader shifts into a *facilitation* mode.

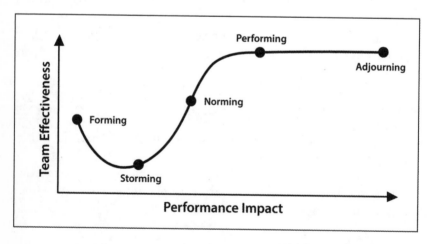

FIGURE 9.1   The Five Stages of Team Development

The **Norming** stage takes place when agreement and consensus emerge among the team. Roles are now clear and accepted, a coherent approach takes shape, and team "chemistry" begins to form.

Then they move into **Performing.** The team begins to collaborate to develop and work the plan. Disagreements are resolved within the team positively. Members of the team operate fairly independently of the leader, whose role shifts to *overseeing* and coordinating the project.

The **Adjourning** phase occurs when the project has been completed. Before the team breaks up, project leaders *celebrate* their team and host a closure event.

Your aim is to move from forming to performing as smoothly and quickly as possible, while ensuring that the interpersonal bonds are built, and a sound plan is developed. The LogFrame supports these phases by providing a structure to guide conversations, efficiently share ideas, and create an executable plan.

Create a Start-Up LogFrame

A proven front-end tool to get your project moving is . . . guess what . . . a *startup* LogFrame! This type of LogFrame highlights the broader tasks and issues needed to get the project off the ground. The example in Figure 9.2 has six Outcomes, but only Outcome #3 is about creating the project LogFrame itself, to be done with the team. This LogFrame is for your own strategizing, and you can share with others or not.

Prepare for a Productive Project Launch

Modify the following steps as needed to get the smooth start you are looking for, one that builds commitment and momentum while aligning the team.

1. Scope Out the Broader Context

When you first receive a project (or create your own), begin by understanding where and how it fits within the larger organization context; how it will support the business area it falls within; and what cultural and political aspects are important to factor into your project.

Objectives	Success Measures
Goal: Successful Project	1. Project meets identified Objectives on-time and within budget. 2. Team enjoys the experience: learns, grows, and feels satisfied. 3. All key stakeholders are pleased.
Purpose: Team gets smooth, quick start.	Within _____ days of formation, team develops and agrees on approach in Start-Up LogFrame, then accepts their task responsibilities and is active in implementing them.
Outcomes: 1. Project Team formed and functioning	1.1 Key team members identified and recruited by _____. 1.2 Team formed and holds initial meeting by _____. 1.3 Team modifies and develops this or similar Pre-Project LogFrame by _____.
2. Stakeholder analysis completed	2.1 Key players and their interests identified by _____. 2.2 Decisions made about who to include in developing the project LogFrame and how to involve other stakeholders.
3. Initial project LogFrame developed	3.1 By _____, team constructs first cut LogFrame for the project. 3.2 LogFrame includes Objectives, Measures, Assumptions, and Tasks, and meets quality standards for a good LogFrame (see checklist in Appendix).
4. Supporting tools and processes developed	4. Team creates WBS, Gantt charts, and/or Responsibility Charts as needed by _____.
5. Execution and monitoring system in place	5. Team decides on how they will monitor progress, report to others, adjust plans, etc.
6. (Other Outcomes as needed)	

FIGURE 9.2 Example Start-Up LogFrame

While some of the context information will be found in documents like the business case (if one was created), greater insight comes through consulting with your senior-level stakeholders. Some questions to help assess the context are below:

- Why do this project now? What is the history behind it?
- How does it fit into the larger program or strategic portfolio?
- What is the level of urgency behind it?
- Which stakeholders have legitimate power and influence over the project?
- What is the order of most essential: time, money, quality, or scope?
- What are the boundaries, risks, and constraints?
- Will you be assigned a team, or must you recruit?
- How will success be measured and by whom?

Begin your stakeholder consultations well prior to the project kick-off to understand their expectations and prevent surprises. Avoid having to regroup after a kick-off meeting that did not go well.

After this consultation, you can begin to assemble a rough draft LogFrame of what you envision as the project strategy, given your current understanding. Take a stab at identifying the Goal and Purpose, and the associated Measures, along with the main tasks and risks. Get feedback from your senior stakeholders. Alternatively, you can wait until the project design workshop when the core team is in place.

2. Recruit and Engage Your Core Team

Core team members are your backbone of trusted players needed to get the ball rolling and keep it rolling. Who are they in your case? Sometimes they are assigned; in other cases you must recruit. You do not need to identify every team member at once, but you should find a few sparkplugs early on. Here are some questions to answer as you put together your team:

- Who has the technical skills needed to get the job done?
- What other skills or perspectives do we need, and who has them?

- Who would it be smart to include for political reasons?
- Whose involvement would give the project greater credibility and visibility?
- Who gives us access to information and other resources?
- For each potential person, what is their track record as a team player?

Map out the key players, identify the working relations needed, and build out the core team. Whether they are assigned or you are able to choose, connect with each individual. Describe what the project is all about, explain why you want them on your team, and ask for their help. Build positive working relations from day one.

Once you brief your team on their mission (should they choose to accept it), you are ready for the project design workshop.

Conduct a Project Design Workshop

Get your core team together and follow the application steps from Chapter 4 through Chapter 8. Invite the sponsor or a senior person to kick off the session.

Make sure everyone is familiar with these planning concepts, by reading this book, reviewing training materials, or being briefed by you. And if you get a question and are unsure of the answer, I would be happy to help. You can find my contact information following Chapter 12.

If meeting in person, gather your team in a conference room where you can write ideas on a whiteboard or put sticky notes on a wall and then populate the LogFrame cells.

Be guided by the now-familiar four questions covered earlier. When the first three questions have been adequately addressed, proceed to map out an action plan that identifies tasks, schedule, and responsibilities. This is where project planning software can be very helpful.

When the LogFrame has been completed to the team's satisfaction, your team along with key decision makers can then choose to: (1) move ahead with the project with strategies to minimize risk or have contingency plans in place; (2) move forward to a more rigorous analysis; (3) modify the project; (4) postpone the decision; or (5) choose not do the project.

If you cannot huddle your team around a whiteboard, go virtual.

Virtual Online LogFrame Design Tips

Well-designed and facilitated virtual planning sessions can be highly effective. Michael Fraidenburg, author of *Mastering Online Meetings*, offers the following tips.

Set up your emerging LogFrame in an online document or on a virtual whiteboard so team members can collaborate and edit the same document. This emulates the process of the team gathering in front of a whiteboard to co-edit the same LogFrame.

Ensure everyone can share text documents, spreadsheets, surveys, and polls as needed. And consider investing in mind-mapping software that supports shared authoring to brainstorm and organize ideas that feed into the LogFrame.

Ideally, each remote team member should have two computer monitors. That way they can have video conferencing open on one monitor and their shared LogFrame and other documents open on the second monitor.

Some discussions are just too long, too complex, or too involved to do in a real-time video conference. Yet teams may need the ability to share considerable detail before they coalesce on a consensus decision. Fortunately, there are *asynchronous* tools like blogs, wikis, and discussion boards that meet this need. They allow all team members to visit and work on the project, but at different times. And these give you the chance to host a meeting-before-the-meeting.

It is remarkable how much more productive teams become when they collaboratively flesh out their project strategy using online team canvas software or a wall-size LogFrame grid. Try it and discover this for yourself.

Engage a Neutral Facilitator

For strategically significant, complex, costly, or politicized projects, it is wise to bring in an outside facilitator who has LogFrame knowledge and project design experience to guide your design meetings. The right person will have communication skills so they can ensure conversation clarity and completeness, conflict-resolution skills so they can mediate agreement and closure, a wide array of process tools so they can adapt the process to meet the team's needs, and just enough knowledge of the project so they can keep up with the team while remaining neutral about the content. This upfront investment will pay handsome dividends in getting a smooth start and reducing costly headaches down the road.

Hold a Project Kickoff Meeting

Plan your kickoff (launch) event to engage and involve a larger group. Attendees include core team members, of course, along with senior leaders, subject matter experts, support personnel, implementors, and other stakeholders who will be involved in implementation.

Present the LogFrame from the design meeting. If you have done a good job in soliciting inputs from the key stakeholders, there will not be much disagreement or change to the basic strategy your plan maps out.

Your aim is to build shared understanding support for your project from all stakeholders the start. For a deeper dive into this topic, refer to *Project Kickoff: How to Run a Successful Kickoff Meeting in Easy Steps* by Hassan Osman.

Design your kickoff to cover topics such as:

- Project Objectives and Measure of success
- Team members and structure
- Roles and responsibilities
- High-level schedule
- Significant findings from the business case
- Scope and boundaries
- Communication plan
- Major Assumptions and risk-management plan
- Information sharing and reporting
- Constraints and dependencies
- Resources and budget
- Technology tools to be used
- Change management process and escalation path
- Decision-making authorities
- Project relationship to larger program
- Company dynamics that may influence

Engage Your Stakeholders Early

People support what they help create, so engage key stakeholders early. Ask the following questions to identify who they are.

- Who are we doing this for? (customers or end-users)
- Who really wants to see this happen? (champions)
- Who might oppose? (blockers)
- Who else does its affect? (indirect beneficiaries and/or victims)
- Whose expertise and support do we need to execute the project? (implementors)
- What resources do we need, and who controls them? (gatekeepers and enablers)
- Who is paying for this effort? (sponsors)
- Who would it be smart to include for political reasons?
- Whose involvement would give the project greater credibility and visibility?

Analyze Stakeholder Interests

Your aim is to build support for your project from the start. Use a stakeholder analysis matrix as shown in Figure 9.3 to guide you.

Start by identifying, as best you can, each stakeholder's issues and interest concerning the project.

Stakeholder	Issues & Interest	Degree of Support Needed			Degree of Support Predicted		
		Crucial	Somewhat	Not Needed	Strong	Neutral	Opposed

FIGURE 9.3   Stakeholder Analysis Matrix

Then, identify the degree of support you *need* from each stakeholder, and the degree of support you *predict* you will have. Further discussions may be required to determine this. From there you can decide how to best involve each person in the initial planning and subsequent stages.

Look for gaps between the support you need and the support you predict. If a stakeholder's support is crucial or somewhat important, but you predict neutral support or outright opposition, your options are to:

- *Enroll them*—Get them enthused about the vision.
- *Convince them*—Use reasoned discourse.
- *Accommodate them*—Incorporate their concerns into your solution.
- *Trade them*—Commit to "owing them one" in the future.
- *Pressure them*—Use legitimate power to reduce resistance.
- *Love them*—Use your winning personality to smother them in goodwill.

If these approaches do not work, your remaining options are to:

- *Moot them*—Make them irrelevant by insulating the project from their nonsupport.
- *Ignore them*—Acknowledge their concerns but press ahead anyway.

In Figure 9.4 is a stakeholder analysis for the Asian Gypsy Moth case study, which we covered in Chapter 7.

The governor and agriculture industry fully supported the project. Ecologists, who might have stopped the project, were united in their desire to rid the beautiful Northwest of this pest, and doing it without using damaging insecticides.

But several troubling gaps appeared in the degree of support needed. Legislator support was crucial, but initially predicted as neutral, because the lawmakers did not yet understand the urgency. This pinpointed a need to brief them personally and win their active support.

There was also a support gap for the general public. Their support was vital, since low-flying helicopters would soon buzz their

Stakeholder	Interests & Issues	Degree of Support Needed			Degree of Support Predicted		
		Crucial	Some-what	Not Needed	Strong	Neutral	Opposed
1. Governor's Office	Minimize active public opposition.	X			X		
2. Legislators	Represent constituent interests. Visible, active oversight.	X				X	
3. Dept. of Health	Ensure safety and health.		X			X	
4. Agriculture Industry	Minimize costs to farmers.	X			X		
5. WSDA Personnel Dept.	Hire necessary staff.	X				X	
6. Ecologists	Restore healthy interaction webs. Minimize "collateral" damage to non-target species.		X		X		
7. Butterfly collectors	Minimize "collateral" damage to non-target species.		X				X
8. General Public	Be safe.	X					X
9. Media	Inform the public.	X				X	
10. Moths	Survive!			X			X

FIGURE 9.4   Stakeholders Analysis of the Asian Gypsy Moth Project

neighborhoods and spray a mysterious mist. Media cooperation was essential to educate citizens about the seriousness of the problem without triggering a panic. Butterfly collectors, a politically influential group, initially opposed the effort, but lent support after the project team added funds to restock the butterfly population.

One group in particular strongly opposed the project: the moths. Fortunately, their support was not required.

Create a High-Performance Culture

Team culture and chemistry can make or break a project. Therefore, it is well worth investing time and effort to build good vibes starting on day one. Get to know each team member and help build supporting relationships among them. Working on a team that enjoys being together and accomplishing great things is rewarding for all.

Include in your early meetings a discussion of what best practices and norms the team will follow in working together. Do not grab off-the-shelf lists of best practices. Instead, grow your own by drawing on your team's experience. Follow the lead of Hewlett-Packard's Joe Cronin, who admits his flubs from his early days. He then asks team members for what worked in their most successful and satisfying projects. The group distills these down and commits to follow these practices. People then own the results. This buy-in process helps build the psychological trust discussed earlier and generates *esprit de corps*.

Make Responsibilities Clear

The Saga of the Confused Project Team

Four people named Everybody, Somebody, Anybody, and Nobody worked together. An important Outcome needed managing, and Everybody was sure that Somebody would do it. Anybody could have done it, but Nobody actually did it. Somebody got angry, because it was really Everybody's job. Everybody thought Anybody could do it, but Nobody realized that Somebody would not. As it turned out, Everybody blamed Somebody when Nobody did what Anybody could have done!
—Author Unknown

Sound familiar? Blame, wasted effort, and sour feelings occur when something important drops through the cracks due to poor communication or faulty coordination. Sorting out roles and responsibilities is tricky when tasks involve multiple people, as they usually do. Fortunately, there is a simple tool to assist us: The Linear Responsibility Chart (LRC) as shown in Figure 9.5. The LRC is an expanded version of commonly used RACI Charts (Responsible, Accountable, Consulted, Informed.)

Linear Responsibility Chart General Format

Inputs	Responsibilties						Responsibility Code
Action Steps:	Name	Name	Name	Name	Name	Name	R = Responsible to do P = Participates C = May be Consulted I = Must be Informed A = Approves

FIGURE 9.5   The Linear Responsibility Chart Shows Actions and Actors

An LRC shows:

- All tasks or action steps (along the vertical axis).
- All persons or organizations involved in the project (along the horizontal axis).
- The responsibilities of all persons in the project task (by a letter code in cells of the matrix).

Use this simple letter code to identify responsibilities of each player:

R: Responsible to do (but may delegate)
P: Participates
C: May be **C**onsulted
A: Approves
I: Must be **I**nformed

You can easily convert the LRC into narrative job descriptions for each person or project entity.

Clarify Decision Rights

Reduce a major potential conflict source early by establishing who makes certain decisions of what types, and who can influence those decisions. Being clear about decision right avoids the confusion, frustration, and misunderstanding as in the Abbott and Costello "Who's on first?" comedy routine.

When to Pivot Your Strategy

The ability to pivot your business or operation is a true competitive advantage, whether forced by external circumstances, or as a proactive decision. Some necessary reasons for a strategy update include:

- **The market has sharply changed.** You are losing customers, and an urgent, well-conceived pivot is needed because of disruptive technology, a smart competitor, pandemic, or other unpleasant surprises.
- **Your current strategies have gone stale.** Like homemade bread, the useful life of strategies decays over time. If they are not producing results, turn up the oven to 350 degrees, and bake a fresh batch.
- **New leaders have come on board.** They bring fresh perspectives and vision along with blind spots. Integrate their vision with what exists.
- **Loss of focus.** An old proverb reminds us a person who chases two rabbits will lose both. Simplify and focus on doing what you do best.
- **Pressure.** Customers, senior management, or your upset boss expect more from your operation. You feel the burn and must deliver results.

Thus far in the book we have discussed the LogFrame from a project or program design perspective. But it can also be used to upgrade, pivot, or transform performance at the enterprise, department, group, or team level with a "Quick and Clean" (as opposed to "quick and dirty") strategy refresh process.

This eight-step process begins with a situation analysis, and results in a carefully defined set of action initiatives. The bonus materials outline these steps in detail and offers tips on how to apply them. The following section highlights selected portions of the analysis and shows how the LogFrame supports organization unit reinvention.

Case Study: Upgrading Group Performance

The Los Alamos National Laboratory (LANL) is an 8,000+ person U.S. government research institute spread out over a rugged mountainous area in northern New Mexico. LANL is responsible to:

- Ensure the safety and reliability of the U.S. nuclear weapons stockpile
- Develop technical means for reducing the global threat of weapons of mass destruction or terrorism
- Solve national problems in energy, environment, infrastructure, health and security

The Geographic Information Systems (GIS) Team at LANL is a 25-person group that produces sophisticated and customized maps of the reservation for various Lab customers.

The importance of GIS services became clear during a devastating wildfire that raced across the Lab, burning over 500 homes and threatening critical Lab facilities. GIS was called on and worked 24/7 to provide maps to firefighters in this fast-breaking situation. Though the team delivered, the chaotic experience revealed serious shortcomings in how they operated. They recognized an urgent need to improve.

The GIS director invited me to facilitate a two-day planning workshop. He would soon leave to take on a larger role and wanted to ensure that his team had the necessary procedures and processes in place in order to deliver superior products and services.

Localize the Mission

It is valuable for any organization unit to periodically revisit, refine, and perhaps redefine *Why* they exist. I call this *localizing the mission* and this is particularly important in large organizations where the connection between the contribution of any particular work unit to the whole organization is unclear, unmeasurable, or suboptimum. The larger the pivot required, the more vital this step becomes.

The same causal logic that aligns Objectives in project Log-Frames also applies to any organization unit. After lively discussion, the GIS team crafted a Goal and Purpose statement covering their operational unit as follows:

Goal:
Internal customers are **satisfied** with and *use* GIS-provided products and services to make informed decisions that support good environmental stewardship of the lab.

Purpose/Mission:

To efficiently *provide* various decision makers with needed map products and services that meets their needs.

Note the clear causal relationship between these two Objectives—If we *provide*, *Then* customers will *use*. Also note that they are easily measurable. The team chose a few key indicators for each of these major Objectives, along with three additional Objectives/Measures (shown in Figure 9.6 the matrix ahead).

Identify Problems and Develop Solution Strategies

In a lively and psychologically safe session, the team identified these critical interrelated problems needing resolution:

- There is no common way of doing maps.
- Team members are dispersed to customer sites, and they seldom meet together.
- There is low morale.
- Potential lab customers are not knowledgeable of GIS's existence and their products.
- Some data used in maps is out of date.
- There are widely varying skills, with no formal way to enhance employee skills.

The team concluded that their root cause problem was the lack of standard operating procedures and processes for doing effective work and enhancing staff satisfaction.

Next came the most creative part—crafting strategies to improve/impact those chosen Objectives/Measures. After spirited discussion, the team identified eight core strategies that would reduce these problems and impact the success measures:

1. **Conduct of Operations**

   Improve formality of team operations and standardize procedures and data.

2. **Data of Known Accuracy and Lineage**

   Ensure that data has appropriate metadata attached and customers are aware of limitations.

3. **Continuous Process Improvement**

Continually improve team processes and services.

4. **Marketing**

Enhance team visibility and customer base via web page and information program.

5. **Customer Feedback**

Monitor customer satisfaction through surveying and analyzing lessons learned.

6. **Customer Education**

Educate customers about the products and services we have to offer.

7. **Team Networking**

Improve team dynamics through meetings, periodic get-togethers, and networking with other LANL GIS nodes.

8. **Employee Development**

Enhance development of technical and management skills, through formal and informal means.

Note how each of these strategies is stated in a brief title, followed by a one-sentence description that makes it easy to understand. Further elaboration of each strategy would be provided by the LogFrames developed for each strategy.

Develop a Measures/Strategy Matrix

Now let us introduce an innovative and underutilized analysis tool. The Success Measures/Core Strategies matrix shown in Figure 9.6 offers a practical method for aligning the strategies needed to impact the desired measures. This is Step 4 in the process.

The left vertical column summarizes the key success measures identified for the GIS unit. They consisted of the Goal and Purpose statements, plus three other priority Objectives. The horizontal axis states each of the strategies. Developing this matrix is a creative and iterative process of identifying potential strategies and testing their impact on the measures. Checkmarks in the cells indicate the degree of impact of each strategy on each measure.

Then, for each of the eight strategies, the team created a simple LogFrame. Various team members stepped up to "own" each

✓✓ = Major Impact   ✓ = Some Impact

KEY SUCCESS MEASURES	CORE STRATEGIES							
	1. Conduct of Operation	2. Team Networking	3. Continuous Process Improvement	4. Marketing	5. Customer Feedback	6. Customer Education	7. Data of Known Accuracy & Lineage	8. Employee Development
1. Customer Satisfaction with quality of GIS products and services	✓✓	✓	✓✓		✓	✓		
2. Efficiently provide our customers with needed services and products		✓		✓	✓	✓		
3. Greater team cohesiveness, and living our values	✓		✓				✓	✓
4. Effective and consistent utilization of best practices	✓✓		✓			✓	✓	
5. Increased Division and Lab awareness of Team services and products				✓✓		✓		

FIGURE 9.6   GIS Success Measures/Strategy Matrix

strategy. They then prioritized and implemented these at a rate of two per quarter, so as not to overwhelm the staff or interfere with ongoing operations.

You can easily adapt this flexible process to meet your own needs.

An Unsolicited Letter That Made My Day

Management consultants like myself get warm and fuzzy feelings when a client sends an unexpected letter to report a success story. GIS team member Tony Tagliaferro made these observations in an email sent to me a year after the workshop.

> During these workshops, the folks in the GIS group came together and focused on a specific direction. We had become overwhelmed and disillusioned by the weight of the organization and allowed the bureaucracy to make us feel powerless and not able to get things done. But after the workshop, we felt empowered and in control. Our perception of upper management improved, and things went smoother. We worked better as a team. Our morale and performance improved dramatically.

Tony's letter confirmed what a motivated group of men and women can do when they have the right tools and are empowered by their leaders to shape their own destiny.

Review Key Points

1. Prepare to launch your project by first identifying where and how it fits into its larger context. Consult with senior-level stakeholders to learn more about what they envision as the Objectives.

2. Size up your stakeholders, their interests, and their degree of support. Bring key players on board during plan creation because people who perceive themselves as co-creators are more positively involved and committed. If you find a gap between needed and predicted support, use your influence to close that gap.

3. Hold a project design workshop. Use the LogFrame process to guide team conversations in a way that efficiently surfaces issues to help create agreement and quickly pinpoint areas of disagreement.

4. Conduct a kickoff meeting attended by all relevant parties to get the project going with clarity and commitment.

5. When circumstances require a change in strategy or direction, follow the eight-step pivot process to get back on the right track.

Coming Up Next

In the next chapter you will learn how to leverage your inner thoughts and emotions as a project resource, to produce positive results for both you and your team. You will learn about your "Internal Operating System" or IOS, how to quickly detect and head off negative emotions and thoughts as they start, and quickly move out of those states to more productive ones. Having the courage to expand your "comfort zone" provides the self-confidence you will need to inspire your team to take on new challenges themselves.

10

Managing Your Inner Game

One can have no smaller or greater mastery than mastery of oneself!

—Leonardo da Vinci

You may have the perfect plan, but your ability to deliver it relies heavily on your ability to direct, lead, and inspire. These skills are not rooted in your technical skills, but in your mindset and "heart-set"—your inner game, if you will.

During every project journey, there will be people and events that trigger negative emotions in you. How you handle yourself in those situations can make the difference between a harmonious project and one that frustrates everyone involved.

What strategies are available to remain calm, centered, and productive, regardless of the noise around us? How can you more easily step into higher performance states? How can you leverage the internal mental and emotional assets you already have in order to handle any personal and interpersonal challenges you may face?

This chapter explores these topics and offers strategies that will not only make you a better project leader, but a better human being.

Leverage Your Internal Operating System

Here is a proposition you can test for yourself: To better manage projects, you need to better manage other people. To better manage other people, you need to better manage yourself. To better manage yourself, you need to better manage your *Internal Operating System*, or your IOS.

The human mind has been compared to a highly sophisticated computer, but it does not come with a manual. Using a vastly simplified metaphor, your IOS consists of your thoughts, emotions, and physiology in real time. The intersection of these three factors generates what we call our present state, as shown in Figure 10.1.

Your mental and emotional wiring can get corroded, burned out, short-circuited, and it can result in degraded performance unless we take steps to refresh and leverage these basic operating elements.

Your present state determines the range of behavioral options available to you at any point in time. The behaviors you choose— your words, actions, and interactions—impact the results you get.

By learning to be consciously aware of your present state in real time, you gain the power to make better choices and decisions about how to act in any situation.

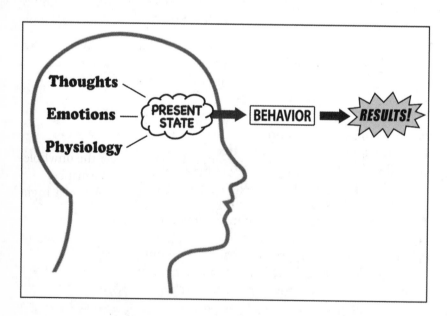

FIGURE 10.1 Your Present State Impacts Your Results

If you are angry with someone, your readily available behavior choices are limited to harsh words and actions. But calming yourself can enable you to be more reasonable and to resolve the issues without resentment. With practice, you can learn to consistently put yourself into the most useful state at any time to deal with the situation at hand.

Step into Productive States

One highly productive performance state is *relaxed focus*. That is where your thoughts and feelings are aligned with what is most important at the moment, and you get stuff done. Sure, there may be interruptions, and problems may pop up, but you have the capacity and emotional resilience to handle them with ease.

Athletes like to use the phrase *getting in the zone*, and they use triggering devices and words to get into that relaxed focus state. Larry Bird, the great basketball player of the Boston Celtics, said that when he was in the zone, it seemed as though he could see the entire court at once and the whole game slowed down. This enabled him to do anything he wanted to do. Rod Carew, the baseball batting great, said when he was in the zone, the ball looked as big as a grapefruit, and he could not miss hitting it cleanly.

Being in a relaxed focus zone lets you interpret situations more objectively, so you can handle difficult decisions and difficult people with greater grace and effectiveness.

You have been in that state many times before. Recall one now. What were you doing at the time? What were you thinking or saying to yourself? What emotions did you feel? Did you sense a certain upbeat cadence within you?

You can learn to condition yourself to get to any state more often by using anchors and reminders. Anchor yourself with positive, uplifting, and powerful thoughts, and remind yourself to reject the unwholesome, unhealthy, and fearful thoughts that stifle your performance.

What's the key to more consistently unlocking your own high-performance states? It begins with how you think.

Take Charge of Your Thoughts

Take a moment to ask yourself, *What am I thinking about or saying to myself right now?* Perhaps your conversation concerns the ideas you are reading as you think about them. But until you paid attention to it right now, it's possible your thoughts have flashed backward to a pleasant memory or forward to some upcoming event.

Thoughts and emotions mesh together like gears in a transmission. Shifts in either thoughts or emotions can immediately impact the other characteristic and determine your internal state and performance capacity.

Talk Nice to Yourself

We all have an ongoing inner dialogue that runs 24/7. It has been estimated we feed ourselves 20,000 messages a day, with most of it repeating what we heard before.

Much of this self-talk occurs below the level of conscious awareness, but this chatter gobbles up mental and emotional bandwidth we could otherwise use more productively.

Your ability to talk to yourself constructively and to quickly replace sidetracking emotions with productive ones opens the channels to deliver better results with greater ease. That's power.

Two common internal voices are those of our *critic* and of our *cheerleader*.

Your inner critic sends you discouraging messages . . . You can't do that . . . they will never believe you . . . you are too young/old to be taken seriously . . .you will fail . . . you are not smart enough . . . blah blah blah. Put downs and trash talk are the critic's specialty, especially when we face situations outside of our comfort zone.

But the critic is just to protect us from potential pain or disappointment. The problem is not the constant chatter, the problem is we frequently believe the chatter is true. You can learn to turn down the volume of the inner critic or ignore it entirely.

The opposite voice is that of our cheerleader. That's the gentle voice that is compassionate towards you and others as well. It affirms you, encourages you, and loves you. This voice on your side, honoring who you are, congratulating your simple victories and encouraging you through any struggles you face.

You feel the cheerleader's presence when reading an inspirational book, walking in nature, or snuggling with your pet. It whispers in moments of reverie or prayer and reminds you that you are beautiful, magnificent, and capable of handling whatever comes up.

While the critic jumps in without being asked, like that annoying donkey in *Shrek*, engaging the cheerleader requires making a special invitation. Which one do you listen to most often? And which do you speak to more often? It is your choice.

Appraise and Reframe the Situation

When something disturbing happens, recognize that it is not the event per se that causes you to feel good or bad. Rather, it's how you appraise or interpret the event that determines your emotional reaction. Nobody can make you mad without your permission.

Your emotional reaction depends heavily on how you frame (interpret) the issue. Your initial thoughts might see it one way, but there are other ways to see the situation. Reframing your thoughts about a problem situation gives you fresh new lenses through which to view the situation. Use the "maybe-but-maybe" reframe pattern to consider other possibilities.

- Maybe the real problem is not the decision they made, maybe the real problem is how I heard about it.
- Maybe the real problem is not her lack of enthusiasm, maybe the real problem is how I am communicating with her.
- Maybe the real problem is not the project sponsor, maybe the real problem is I never talk to them about the difficulties I'm having.
- Maybe the real problem is not_____, maybe the real problem is _____.

Inaccurate or self-defeating interpretations do not serve you. It's always best to assume good intent on the part of others. By reframing, you will see you are no longer stuck in a rut, but are on your way to finding an effective behavioral response to a challenging situation.

Recognize it is your own thoughts, emotions and physiological changes (your own IOS)—and nothing else—that drive your behavioral responses. Realize you can take control of these by first being aware of them and then by reframing the situation.

Manage Your Emotions

When dealing with any emotion, in all cases the first step is to acknowledge the emotion without making yourself wrong. All emotions are valuable because they provide actionable signals that something needs attention; suppressing or denying them does not work because they fester. The key is to understand the message your emotion is giving you.

When a strong emotion like anger or fear comes up, it is too easy to get caught up in the energy of the emotion itself, rather than calming down, so you can rationally explore the message the emotion offers. What is this emotional signal trying to tell you? What's the underlying problem? What's the action you need to take? Use your problem-solving skills to come up with an action plan.

Handling tough issues often requires interacting with others in ways that can be uncomfortable. Prepare yourself for difficult conversations by rehearsing instructional self-statements. These are messages you give yourself that boost your courage . . . I can deal with this . . . I can find the right way to say it without causing resentment . . . We will all feel better when it's handled. Preparation also means anticipating their reaction, and holding the other person in high regard while focusing on the issue.

One effective way to purge useless noise from your IOS and regain emotional bandwidth is to drop any grudges or lingering resentments about people or past events you may have. It does no good to carry them forward. They are heavy. They drag you down. Forgive others even if *they* do not deserve it. Forgive them because *you* deserve it.

In her book *Molecules of Emotion: The Science Behind My Mind-Body Medicine*, Dr. Candace B. Pert shares her story and the evolution of her thinking. She wrote: "It is the emotions, I have come to see, that link mind and body . . . the molecules of emotion run every system in our body." Her systems thinking came to include other people, the larger environment, and spirituality. She encouraged people to take on emotional self-care—acknowledging and claiming all emotions, not just the "acceptable" or "positive ones"—and then let them go. Regarding interpersonal relations, Pert wrote: "The emotions are the connectors, flowing between individuals, moving among us as empathy, compassion, sorrow and joy."

Manage Your Physiology

Physiology completes the IOS triad. Managing your physiology means being aware of and intentional about how you are using your body. Subtle changes in your heart rate, breathing, sweating, and facial flush are leading indicators of emotional state changes. By noticing these early indicators, you can center yourself, which in turn helps you think clearly and behave in a way that matches your Objectives.

Personally, when I am in a conversation and notice I am speaking louder and faster and that my cheeks begin to warm, that is a leading indicator I am getting angry. That awareness lets me remind myself it is time to take a deep breath and slow down.

Managing your physiology can also help you break out of gloomy moods or "stuck states." Stuck states are when you have fallen into a dull funk for some reason. You would like to shake out of it, but do not have the mental or emotional energy to do so.

The formula you need to quickly and easily break out of stuck states is to *get up and move your body*. Run around the block or in place. Breathe deeply five times. Do a dozen jumping jacks. Laugh crazily like a hyena. Get on the floor and play with your pet. Dance wildly to your favorite music. Shake-shake-shake to get your mojo back on track.

To deepen your inner skills, check out the books written by Dr. Hendrie Weisinger. This two-time *New York Times* best-selling author's books include *The Power of Positive Criticism*; *Performing Under Pressure*; *Emotional Intelligence at Work*; and *Push: The Unlikely Art of Positive Parental Pressure*.

Strengthen Your Courage Muscles

I believe than the number one thing holding people back from being an outstanding project leader, or experiencing a full and rich life, is fear.

But our fight-or-flight response cannot tell the difference between real danger, imagined danger, or an unfamiliar situation. We get trapped by the imagined hurt or pain we do not want to experience.

Personal growth only occurs outside of our comfort zones. Yet we hesitate to step out of the zone because of the imagined hurt or pain it will bring. We sense danger. So, we do not ask for that raise. We do not report a problem because we are afraid of the other person's reaction. Better to play it safe and avoid the pain our inner critic says.

But beyond the boundaries of our comfort zone is an *innovation laboratory*, where you can experience, discover, and grow.

Courage is the antidote to fear, and courage comes by taking action. The smartest way to strengthen courage muscles is to *feel the fear and do it anyway*. Here is one way to condition yourself to fear less.

Get Yourself Rejected!

Twice a year, I teach a course at the UCLA Extension Technical Management Program called *Reinvent Yourself and Thrive*. The course is all about exploring the inner self and creating a more empowering identity.

The audience is typically comfortable with facts and equations, but skeptical about the "touchy-feely" stuff. Since they are brave enough to enroll, my job is to create a transformational experience that lets them break through imagined barriers.

The homework on the first night is to ask a total stranger for something and get rejected. Yes, get rejected. The wilder the request, the better. They can approach whomever they want, and ask for anything sure to generate a NO answer. When they get rejected, they simply thank the person. Getting rejected was their win.

The class was clearly hesitant, but the next day they reported back and shared their requests with great enthusiasm. Would you please give me $100? Can I borrow your car this weekend? Can I try your shoes? If they got a YES, they failed the assignment.

To pull this off, they needed to dial up their courage level and ignore the inner voice whispering it is too scary. But when they successfully pulled it off, they felt energized and alive!

Their internal beliefs shifted. They learned getting a no did not mean being rejected as a person. Instead of the pain and embarrassment they feared, they knew they could handle any temporary embarrassment or criticism, and became stronger as a result.

Build Your Emotional Resilience

I believe the ability to maintain a positive charge in our lives and be an example to others relies on our emotional resilience. Emotional resilience means the ability to respond and turn setbacks into comebacks. Consider these strategies to condition yours.

Care More Deeply About Yourself

Develop greater compassion and love for yourself. It's easy to put ourselves down for mistakes and shortcomings. We all do that, but why? The more you care for yourself, the more you are capable of caring about others, and the richer life becomes. Drop the shame and guilt. Invite affirming conversations with your cheerleader and ignore the critic. Be your own best friend.

Take care of your physical well-being as well. Make the earth-suit you were issued at birth last you through a long and productive life. Eat right, get enough sleep, exercise and relax so you have the capacity to generate the energy you need. The cigar-smoking comedian George Burns, at the age of 99, admitted had he known how long he would live, he would have taken better care of himself!

Find Your Support Team

Surround yourself with people who tell you how amazing you are. Listen to them and allow yourself to take in what they say. Support and encourage them as well. Are your social networks providing you with the emotional support, inspiration, and guidance you need?

If not, find your tribes. Check out the many in-person and online communities you can join that cover a variety of topics—relationships, business success, project management, outdoor adventures, fitness, meditation, religion, spirituality, social justice and just about everything else.

At a minimum, have a buddy or two you can freely share whatever is going on in your life with, knowing you will not be judged.

Laugh More Often

It is a funny thing, but from a scientific point of view, laughing releases endorphins—hormones and enzymes that make you feel good—as well as help you relax and even heal.

Peak performance specialist Joseph McClelland III advises getting at least five deep belly laughs a day. Find something that triggers your laughter, or laugh with gusto for no good reason.

There's a neurological reason why this peps you up. When you laugh, you breathe more deeply, which oxygenates your system. Hearty laughter is like an energy drink for your brain. Even just smiling releases oxytocin (the love chemical) into your body—try it more often!

Relax to Restore

When feeling anxious, do what a cab driver (Jamie Foxx) does as the movie *Collateral* opens. Foxx notices his passenger's stress and pulls down his car visor to show her a postcard of a beautiful Caribbean island. He explained that when he felt stressed, he mentally goes to his private island.

Whether it be floating on a raft in the ocean, meditating in your flower garden, or playing catch with your dog, choose a favorite private retreat and think of a word or two that triggers feelings of relaxation within it. With practice, pairing the mental image and a phrase with the sense of relaxation allows you to evoke the relaxation response merely by saying the phrase, such as: "Relax," or "Peace of Mind," or the classic "Om."

Prime Yourself for a Great Day

What would happen if when you woke up each day, you took just 10 minutes to make a list, in your mind or on paper, of all the things you are grateful for? All the things you are proud of. What you are most happy about? All the people you love and who love you. What you are most excited about? What you are committed to?

And as you answer to yourself, associate with those emotions and feelings in your mind and heart. This meaningful morning ritual will launch your day with a positive charge. Give it a try for 10 days and see for yourself.

Take Daily Imperfect Action

What are the top three tasks each day that can have the greatest impact on your project success? Do you find yourself procrastinating because these are activities that involve interacting with others in ways that are uncomfortable? If so, the solution is to visualize positive outcomes and prepare yourself with instructional self-statements.

Mark Twain is often credited with the quotes, "Eat a live frog first thing in the morning and nothing worse will happen to you the rest of the day," and "If you have to eat two frogs, eat the biggest one first." Eat all your frogs as early in the day as you can to get them off your plate. Pretty soon they will not taste so bad. It is just like eating frogs, practicing what impacts your success often takes courage. Confront fear in the face by taking uncomfortable and imperfect action.

Take Charge of What You Can

It is understandable to sometimes feel discouraged or even hopeless when you focus on the Volatile, Uncertain, Chaotic, and Ambiguous factors swirling in the environment. While those dynamics are outside of our ability to influence, there is much you can control.

Remember the wise words of American theologian Reinhold Niebuhr, who said, "God grant me the serenity to accept the things I cannot change, the courage to change the things I can, and the wisdom to know the difference."

What's the number one thing you can change? Your inner game and mindset.

Manage Your Internal PROJECTS

As you flow through the day, keep your IOS in a peak performance state by drawing on these characteristics, summarized in the acronym PROJECTS:

Presence—Be fully engaged, actively listening to your inner voice for the thoughts and emotions and concerns when alone or with others. Give up limiting Assumptions of others based upon the past and be attentive to who they are right now. Breathe deeply three times to center yourself and be in the moment.

Resilience—Let go of past disappointments, get over upsets quickly, and see mistakes as learning opportunities. Drop useless mind-chatter. Use setbacks as motivational fuel to do better instead of making it mean there is something wrong with you or others. Turn setbacks into comebacks.

Optimism—Hope for and expect the best outcomes. Hold the Vision of what you and your team can accomplish by working together. Emotions are contagious, and your optimism instills confidence in yourself and others.

Joy—Learn to create joy in yourself for no good reason. Take moments to notice and experience what brings you joy and wonder. Maybe it's the experience of watching others expand their capabilities, taking a minute to go outside to watch a bird flying, or noticing the shape of a leaf. Sometimes a sincere and well-timed compliment can spark joy within others and lift you up as well.

Empathy—Be willing to connect at a heart level and care deeply about yourself and other people. Go beyond surface conversations. Interact mindfully with others, especially when dealing with sensitive matters. They may be carrying heavy burdens of which you are unaware. And most of all, be empathetic with yourself. Practice radical self-compassion and know you are more than enough—much more than enough.

Courage—Be willing to put yourself on the line. Take meaning-ful risks. Be courageous enough to admit mistakes and open up the space for others to acknowledge their mistakes. Be willing to look foolish and get rejected. Climb over, go around or tunnel through each mountain that dares to block your path.

Trust—Trust yourself and believe you have everything you need. Trust others as well and give them space to blossom. Trust that at some level you "know." Trust you will figure out the solutions to any problems. Trust that you matter.

Strength—Develop the inner belief you can handle whatever comes along. Grow bigger than any problems you face. Let every obstacle you overcome make you stronger. Make decisions and develop habits that support the Vision of what is possible for you, your team, your organization, your family, and your country, as well as our shared planet. Be an inspiration to others.

Practicing these qualities will support your lifelong quest for excellence—not just in your project—but in your life as well.

Review Key Points

1. Managing your inner game can make the difference between well-run projects and those that demoralize and fail.
2. Actively manage and productively integrate the three elements of your IOS—thoughts, emotions, and physiology.
3. Learn to manage your emotions as a powerful and produc-tive project resource. Use real-time awareness of your state to increase behaviors that get you where you really want to be,

while decreasing counterproductive thoughts, emotions, and behaviors.

4. Develop greater emotional resilience by caring more deeply about yourself.

5. When emotions, such as anger and anxiety, come up, what counts is how skillfully and swiftly you can accept your emotions and move out of disempowered states to more productive ones. The faster you can manage your emotional dips and get back on track, the more success you will experience with your projects and in life.

6. Learn to relax in the heat of the moment. This starts with recognizing your emotional indicators, the personal cues that tell you it is time to relax. The sooner you recognize these are changing, the faster you can manage your emotions.

7. Each day manage your PROJECTS, both literally and specifically as defined within the acronym.

Coming Up Next

Research has shown team outstanding performance has less to do with who is on the team and more to do with how the team interacts. People want to do meaningful work and do it for people who care about them. We all thrive on overcoming challenges, winning against the odds, being exceptional, and being able to be ourselves at work.

But what is the number-one key indicator of a team that will perform at a high level? You are about to find out.

11

Building Your High-Performing Team

No one can whistle a symphony. It takes a whole orchestra to play it.

—H.E. Luccok

Even the best project plans are of marginal value without a team that everyone wants to be on—where each member feels valued and safe, has a strong sense of belonging, and is acknowledged as being a strong contributor. That's the formula for outstanding performance, and the focus of this chapter.

Commit yourself to building a team with high mutual regard, a team where everyone can find a sense of meaning in their work. Illustrate to each team member how their work matters, coach, and when appropriate, be a mentor.

This chapter's case study shows the power of using simple and meaningful rituals to transform team performance.

Components of a Stellar Team

Google studied 180+ active Google teams to see what made for the most effective teams. They expected to find the best mix of people with the right skill sets and traits would create a stellar team. *To their surprise, who was on the team mattered less than how the team members interacted.*

The following three dynamics set their successful teams apart from the others.

1. Team Members Have Psychological Safety

Psychological safety tops the list for building a high-performance team and underpins all the other factors. When team members feel safe with you and with one another, they can say what they really think. Without this safety net, they may avoid resolving issues with other team members, remain quiet about a personal or project-related problem, withhold an idea out of fear of rejection, or hide mistakes.

Psychological safety also affects your bottom line. Google found that teams with high levels of psychological safety exceeded revenue targets by 17 percent, while teams with low psychological safety fell short by up to 19 percent.

Bring all your inner game elements to build a psychologically safe environment of caring and trust.

- Let team members know you are committed to their success, and what they can count on you for.
- Get to know each one personally, find out what is important to them, and build a caring relationship.
- Let them get to know the real you—warts and all. Be, open, authentic, direct, and warm.
- Keep your promises and clean it up with your team members when you do not.
- Listen with your full attention and with the intention to be a contribution to them.
- Understand and forgive when people make mistakes. Put the focus on learning from mistakes, instead of making people feel bad.

- Be sure everyone is heard.
- Find ways to relate how the project connects with their personal Vision.
- Model the values and behaviors you wish others to practice.

Pay special attention to people working remotely because they can easily feel isolated, stressed, or lonely. They will appreciate you reaching out to them individually with genuine caring. You may choose to start online meetings with a quick round of emotional check-ins.

Heated discussions will sometimes occur among team members who feel psychologically safe enough to fully express their point of view. As long as people are not hurling personal insults or tomatoes at each other, consider tension and disagreement to be part of the team-building process. Studies of great teams have shown they encourage differing opinions. A diversity of perspectives allows for creative and sound solutions. Keep the team focused on their common purpose.

Give the Gift of Grace

What should you do if someone violates your trust? Should you get angry? Avoid them? Retaliate? Let the feelings fester? Carry a lingering resentment? There's a better way. It is called giving *grace*, which is defined as *unmerited favor*.

In his book *R.A.M.P. It Up: 4 Keys to Turbocharge Employee Performance*, Robert Hessler says this about grace: "Used wisely, grace can be the most powerful gesture you can use to build trust. . . It embodies compassion, generosity, and kindness, and when given when someone violates your trust, brings benefits far greater than you might think."

Hessler goes on to list some of the benefits of using grace in the workplace. Grace creates:

- An easier path back to right relationships without awkwardness.
- A channel for quick release of resentment.
- Emotional space to express regret and assurance of better performance.
- More openness about personal issues.

- Most important, grace produces growth. Your actions do not leave people in the same place they started. They become more than they were. And it relieves you of the burden of carrying resentments.

Welcome Diverse Perspectives

Research shows teams perform better and produce richer ideas if they incorporate diverse backgrounds. The more diverse the team, the more you need to help each team member get to know and trust each other. One simple way is during online meetings, invite folks to briefly share a point of interest about themselves or a recent victory. No long stories, just quick thoughts.

2. Team Members Experience Work as Personally Meaningful

Think about the things you enjoy working on, either at home or at work. If you are like most people, what gives you the most satisfaction is working on something important to you that gives you a sense of meaning.

Dr. David Paul, author of *Dare to Care: How High Mutual Regard Increases Engagement and Productivity*, carried out a decade-long research project to discover what really matters to people on teams. "Paul's People Performance Principle," based on his research, states that *people want to do work that matters* for *people who care*. The Marines understand this. That is why they risk their lives to protect their own.

Paul identified 33 categories of statements team members associate with being cared about. The statements with the highest correlation to engagement and connection are below. Do a self-check on your environment and note which of these items are present and which are not.

- I receive professional growth opportunities.
- I feel encouraged and supported.
- I am productive at work.
- I feel important (as in doing work that matters).
- I am given increased responsibility.

- I am allowed to lead.
- My thoughts and opinions are valued.
- I feel a high degree of personal interest in the project or connection to the team.
- I am listened to.

3. Team Members Know the Impact Their Work Creates

People want to know that their work impacts the team, the project, the organization, and the world. Let them know through acknowledgement and celebration.

Acknowledgements are a powerful way to ensure people experience the difference they are making. People love to be recognized for who they are and for their contribution. Acknowledgements make both the acknowledger and the receiver bigger people. This can transform who people are for themselves and others.

For example, "Your commitment to making sure participants in our virtual conference got quick responses to their support requests resulted in our highest participant satisfaction ratings ever. Our company signed up twice as many new customers as was expected for our new software bundle and you really contributed to our great quarterly sales. Well done!"

Find reasons to celebrate success early and often. People love to be recognized for their work. Every worthwhile project has pushed people through frustration, disappointments, setbacks, minor course corrections, and major pivots. But with commitment and encouragement, good people rise to new heights of accomplishment. Recognize and reward team members when the project achieves milestones and when it concludes. Team efforts should be heralded openly, publicly, and joyfully.

Turn WIIFM to WIIFU

Aim to translate team members' focus from *What's In It For Me?* (WIIFM) to *What's In It For Us?* (WIIFU). See the following table for a comparison. Start by meeting with team members individually, learn what they want to achieve, and show them how they might achieve it through the project.

What's In It For Me? (WIIFM)	What's In It For Us? (WIIFU)
• Work on challenging problems	• Be part of something bigger than ourselves as a powerful team
• Get to know other people in the organization	• Bring my unique contributions to the team
• Gain visibility	• Our work enhances the rest of our lives—relationships with family, etc.
• Accomplish something important	• Be rewarded by seeing others grow, knowing we contributed to their growth
• Learn, grow, and gain new skills	
• Get tangible rewards (e.g., bonuses, new opportunities)	
• Experience fun and joy working on this project	• Experience fun and joy working on this team to accomplish its goals
• Have accomplishments I am proud of and am acknowledged for	• Have accomplishments we are proud of and acknowledged for
• My professional growth increases my value	• Enhance our professional value to the current and other organizations

Two additional dynamics made the Google top-five list: (4) dependability, and (5) structure and clarity. Chapter 9 addressed those topics.

Create Engaging Virtual Meetings

Like it or not, virtual meetings are here to stay. So, you might as well get good at them. The people who are best at creating a great virtual meeting experience are highly intentional about making meetings an engaging experience. Here are some tips you may find helpful.

Be clear about the intention of the meeting and what people will get out of it. Prepare focused agendas with clear outcomes. Reserve meetings for discussion and decision making, not for passing along information that can be emailed. Consider that people's attention spans are noticeably short these days—some say eight seconds.

Bring energy and variety to your voice. We are not stuck with the voices we have. According to Roger Love, a world-renowned voice coach for singers and speakers, we have a full range of notes available to us and most of us only use a few "notes" on our "piano." We can do much to vary our melody, pitch, tone, pace, and volume in order to intentionally engage people emotionally.

Be attentive to the other people in the meeting. Pay attention to their faces, tone of voice, and body language. Notice whether they are fully engaged or looking at their phone. Say people's names (we all like to hear our names spoken) and keep the meeting short. Invite questions, call on people, and conclude with action lists.

Bring Humor into Your Meetings

There are many forms of humor. The best humor pokes fun at yourself. Spontaneous humor adds surprise. When you look for ways to add and encourage humor, people will relax and find ways to bring their own humor.

Maybe choose someone to open each meeting with a "dad-joke." These short and lame jokes will elicit a good-natured groan and positive energy. Rotate who the "jokester" is each meeting.

Case Study: Transforming a Team Through Caring

This California nuclear power plant had been closed by the Nuclear Regulatory Commission due to technical violations and faulty construction issues. The necessary repairs went slowly, due to the drafting office staff being slow to issue new blueprints for construction. Mel, an older and quiet man, supervised the drafting office, consisting of men mostly in their mid-twenties. I was asked to be part of a "cultural fix" and began by interviewing the young men.

These young men felt disrespected by Mel, who went straight to his office every morning without giving so much as a nod or a "Hi." And Mel hardly ever smiled. The staff did not feel valued, and this was reflected in their slow and sloppy work. "He does not like us."

Mel was shocked when I told him what his team had shared. "I love these kids. I really care about them. How could they think I don't?" I suggested we all meet in the conference room that afternoon.

Mel was clearly nervous and asked the young men why they felt the way they did. There was silence for a moment. Then, one spoke up. "When you get here in the morning, you go straight to your office and ignore us." Mel fell silent. Then he explained that since he came in later, out of respect, he did not want to disturb them. The young men responded, "but you never smile!"

Tears appeared in the corner of Mel's eyes as he explained something he had never shared before, "My jaw got damaged in the Vietnam War and I literally cannot smile—even when I am happy. But you need to know how proud of you I am."

There was silence for what seemed like a full minute. Then, Mel reached his finger up to his right ear and flicked the lobe twice. "This means I am happy." The staff members smiled, flicked theirs in response, and shortly everyone was laughing, flicking, and feeling happy. A new bonding ritual!

Mel also explained how much their work mattered, using causal language.

"*If* your blueprints are accurate, *Then* the construction team can make repairs. *If* repairs are made, *Then* the plant can reopen. And *If* the plant reopens, *Then* we can provide reliable electricity for the region." Their facial expressions beamed with the pride because they saw how they made a difference.

When I visited a week later, they were doing well. "When Mel comes through in the morning, he flicks his ear, we flick back, and everyone gets a good laugh."

I asked the young men what other issues we should discuss. "Nicknames. Fun at first, but I do not like being called Lazy. Call me 'Roadrunner.'" Then, "Call me 'Einstein' from now on, not 'Dumb-ass,'" and from "Stinky," "Please call me by my real name, Freddy." They all agreed.

Two weeks later, I was welcomed with ear flicks. When I thumped my own ear, we all started laughing. Vibes in the room were different, and productivity had jumped by over 40 percent (as measured by drawings completed each day). People shared that they enjoyed their work again and called Mel the best supervisor ever.

What factors accounted for this dramatic transformation?

Mel's vulnerability and genuine caring created psychological safety. Through uncomfortable conversations, the team discovered the truth. They adopted a fun ritual that generated an upbeat mood and they understood that their work mattered. Everyone involved learned to regard each other with greater respect, love, and appreciation.

For every leader who dares to care, positive results will happen.

Help Others to Become Their Best

No one gets to where they are by themselves. We have all had help along the way. Think back to those from whom you learned great lessons throughout your life. Consider teachers, bosses, colleagues, relatives, religious leaders, business leaders, family members, even characters from literature or movies! You can help others, and be enriched at the same time, by being a coach or mentor, whether in person or not.

Coaches Teach and Guide; Mentors Care and Inspire

I am sure you have experienced the value of having a coach, manager, advisor, or other well-meaning person give you specific and direct guidance. While at first you may not have been happy to hear what they had to say, you became more effective from their feedback and coaching.

Many projects lend themselves to coaching relationships. A team member may request your coaching, or an upper-level manager may request that you coach someone. The best coaching relationships happen when the relationship between coach and subject is open, trusting, and improvement-focused.

Start with an initial meeting to discuss what you are both committed to accomplishing, and establish agreements for how the coaching relationship will work. If you are the coach, ask if you have permission to be direct. Otherwise, he or she may get defensive and become dismissive, or you may hold back from saying what you have to say. Frame feedback from the perspective of your commitment to their growth and development. When given in that context, any feedback can be perceived as constructive and edifying.

Both coaching and mentoring are developmental in nature, but where coaching is performance-oriented, mentors are role models who inspire. A mentor has more of a teacher-student or expert-apprentice relationship, who encourages and suggests new paths for an individual to consider.

We have all had role models who influenced us in some important way. Here is one of mine that demonstrates the life-changing power of just five minutes.

Meeting My Mentor

The following story occurred nearly 50 years ago, but I have never forgotten how you can have an amazing impact on someone's life just by showing them you care.

During my college freshman and sophomore years, fueled by my Rocket Man dream, I sent Dr. von Braun a dozen letters with suggestions for how to build better rockets. My suggestions were naive in retrospect. Each letter received the standard cordial thank-you reply from their press office. But—the letters did get NASA's attention.

As my junior year summer break approached. I wrote von Braun once again, asking for a job. Three weeks later a fat envelope with a NASA return address arrived in the mail. As I eagerly ripped it open and caught a glimpse, I "whooped" at the first sentence: "We are pleased to invite you to be our summer intern!" I was going to assist the *real* engineers by analyzing data from wind tunnel tests.

The highlight of that summer was when I was called into a private meeting with von Braun. I was so excited I bought a brand-new white shirt and the absolute best clip-on tie JCPenney sold! What I experienced that day helped shape my leadership style forever.

Von Braun greeted me like an old friend and shared how his dream of exploring space began as a young boy. In a huge office with dozens of rocket models, he shared his dream of going to the moon and beyond. Von Braun believed with a strong enough vision and a good enough team, you can make anything happen—lessons I have never forgotten. He explained that average engineers become outstanding when they also are skilled in strategy, motivation, influence, teamwork, program management, and communication, and come from a base of strong ethics and values. He asked me questions about my life and goals. He chuckled and congratulated me on my rocket-fish launch. He even took a photo with me, as shown in Figure 11.1. It was clear he cared.

As the hour ended, his assistant opened the door to remind him of another meeting. Von Braun replied to the assistant, "Give me five more minutes with Terry. This is important." Oh, how those

FIGURE 11.1 My Mentor Changed My Life

words inspired me! I choke up even now as I recall the impact those 10 words had on me. My life was changed by his showing he cared about me, and I do my best to pay it forward.

Your Five Minutes Can Change a Life

I believe the best way to honor your coaches, mentors, and heroes is to be grateful for what they instilled in you—and pass it along. Mentoring or coaching others on outside of your team is an opportunity to pass on skills, insights, and wisdom that contribute to the success of your project and their future. Share your gifts with a caring and open heart, and you will gain immense satisfaction. You may even change a life.

Who is someone in your world who needs words of support or inspiration this week?

Review Key Points

1. The heart and soul of every project concerns people—their relationships, skills, and ability to work as a team.
2. Psychological safety is the most important factor to enable team members to trust and perform at their highest level.
3. People want to do work that matters for people who care. If your team feels cared for and are doing work that matters to them, they are likely to engage with passion and commitment.
4. Your team members want their work to have an impact. Acknowledge them frequently and make them aware of the difference they are making for you, for other team members, and for the beneficiaries of the project. Celebrate often and reward the team at key milestones.
5. When doing virtual meetings, be intentional about keeping them short, energetic, and engaging. Use humor. Share stories, both yours and those of others.
6. People thrive on challenges, overcoming obstacles, winning against the odds, and doing an exceptional job. When team members can depend on each other and are rowing in alignment towards a common goal, extraordinary results happen.
7. Seek mentors and coaches for yourself and be that guiding light for others.

Coming Up Next

Now we have examined how to build and energize a committed, passionate team. But what about doing the same for yourself? In the upcoming final chapter, we'll look at how to design your future, craft your vision, build your life project portfolio, and act on it. You'll also explore how to deal with success and failure to help you navigate the path toward your ideal future.

12

Managing Your Life Projects

If you have built castles in the air, your work need not be lost; that is where they should be. Now put the foundations under them.

—Henry David Thoreau, American philosopher

Congratulations on making it to the last chapter—not everyone does. The fact you have stuck with it shows you are a growth-minded, forward-thinking, difference-maker.

I have always believed experiencing a rich and meaningful life doesn't happen by accident. We each have the opportunity to *design* a life, not just *live* one.

Previous chapters covered applying strategic principles and tools to projects at work. Now, in closing, let us apply the same strategic concepts to your life.

While designing a strategy for your life may at first seem like a monumental undertaking, the Logical Framework Approach is your perfect companion that truly allows you to start before you think you're ready.

This chapter reviews the concepts we have learned and considers them as the keystones to your life reimagined, reinvented, and redeveloped into something of incredible value. You might call this *Strategic* Life *Management Made Simple*.

Design Your Future

My first commercially published book, written over 40 years ago, was entitled *Strategic Career Planning for Engineers, Scientists, and Technical Managers*. That is when I first began to apply management principles to the most essential project of all: One's Self.

Virtually everything this book discussed about projects applies to your life as well.

- **The broad organizing principles:** Vision. Objectives. Causality. Chunking. Programs. Projects.
- **The tools to help manage projects:** Objectives Trees. Log-Frames. Measures. Assumptions. Action steps.
- **The process to keep your strategy fresh:** Rolling-wave planning. Strategic Action Cycle. Assessments. Pivoting. Being adaptive.
- **The inner game of head and heart:** Self-awareness. Relaxed focus. Self-compassion. Actively managing the thoughts, emotions, and physiology that make up your Internal Operating System (IOS).
- **The qualities in the PROJECTS acronym:** Presence. Resilience. Optimism. Joy. Empathy. Courage. Trust. Strength.

Projects Are for Life

Are you ambitious and committed to something significant? Are you here to make a difference? Or, as Steve Jobs put it, "put a ding in the universe"? If so, projects can be the force-multipliers to accelerate achieving who you want to become and what you want to accomplish in the world.

Putting the power of projects to work in your own life begins with clarifying your Vision, values, and long-term life goals (or Mission). From these you can derive a set of medium-term goals (three to five years). And from these identify your annual goals. These annual goals can be broken down into short-term Objectives for each quarter or month, with clear measures and milestones to be reached through focused daily action. This cascading set of Objectives constitutes both a roadmap and a strategy guide to your future.

Detailing how to do this requires a book of its own. In this closing chapter we will simply articulate some of the highlights. If you wish to go deeper, you will find personal goal-setting tips in the bonus materials.

Our focus here will be on designing *Life Projects* to be managed with the same care and attention as you would your most essential projects at work.

As you recall, the first step of developing any project is to have a clear idea of your *Why* Goals. So too in your life. Having a working idea of your various life goals gives you the ability to craft the projects to accomplish these goals.

What follows are five steps that take you from Vision to Realization. So, let us begin with the biggest *Why* of the bunch.

Craft Your Personal Vision

As we illustrated in Figure 2.1 in Chapter 2, every organization has a Vision supported by goals and projects. So do each of us in our own way. Gaining clarity about your future Vision can multiply the likelihood you will create the rich life experience you want for yourself and for those you care about.

Think of Vision as your biggest life *WHY*, a Super-Super-Goal of sorts. Your Vision reflects your cherished values and beliefs about what is most important to you. Vision statements express what you were put on earth to do, to become, to experience, to teach, to enjoy, to create, to accomplish, to contribute. A heart-felt Vision statement should inspire positive feelings that get you out of bed in the morning and eager to seize the day.

For this discussion about you and your life, consider the words Vision, Mission, and Life Purpose to mean essentially the same thing: helpful guiding principles that satisfy core values. We will choose to use the terms *Vision* in what follows. Substitute the term *Life Purpose* if you prefer.

Your own Vision may be well-articulated and written down, or it may be a vague. Maybe you are not sure what yours is but you are intrigued to discover it.

In the steps that follow, do not worry about getting these "right"—this is not a test. Just get something down on paper as a start. Have fun with it, be playful and imaginative. This may take more than one sitting, with reflection between sessions. You do not carve a masterpiece out of a mountain in one session. And remember, you can modify your life Vision, goals, strategy, and projects at any time—today, tomorrow, or next year.

Step 1: Draft Your Vision Statement

A simple way to begin is to complete the phrase: The Vision/Purpose of my life is . . .

- To empower people to be heroes—creating a bright future for people, plants, and animals.
- To enroll fearless leaders to fulfill adventurous promises, boldly.
- To enjoy life, make a contribution, and raise a loving family.
- To courageously go where no woman has gone before.
- To use my God-given gifts in every way I can.
- To teach and empower children to be the courageous leaders of the future.

Keep your Vision statement succinct and easy to remember. Write it down. When you recite it aloud, does it have an inspiring ring to it? Play with the phrasing until your words give you an expansive feeling of who you are now and who you are becoming more of each day.

To construct a more comprehensive statement, draw on the connector words from Chapter 3 (by, in order to, so that). For example, the Vision/Purpose of my life is . . .

- To teach and inspire leaders to think bigger, plan smarter, act faster, in order to make a difference in the world.
- To improve the lives of business owners, workers, and their families by creating emotionally healthy, productive, and meaningful workplaces.
- To do the best I can with the resources I have so that I experience a life of meaning and significance.
- To keep vulnerable kids from being bullied by teaching them martial art skills that boost their confidence and ability to fight back when necessary.
- To invent products that make life easier for the elderly so they can experience a higher quality of life.
- To be the trusted advisor, guardian, protector, and supporter for those within my circle of influence through clarity, certainty, consistency, communication, and community.

Internalize the meaning of your words. Keep them visible. Write them in bold colors and tape them to your wall or mirror.

Make them your screen saver. Chant them while exercising, dancing, or listening to your favorite music. Notice how they make you feel. The more you emotionally connect with them, the faster they will become who you are. The second step is to identify potential projects that align with your Vision.

Develop Your Life Project Portfolio

Though it may sound geeky, you can view your life as an ongoing portfolio of programs and projects that evolve during each stage of life. The types of projects vary by life stage: childhood, high school, college, career, first job, and so on. You have already completed many hundreds of successful life projects, whether you called them projects or not, and will continue to do so.

Step 2: Envision Future Possibilities

Put on your long-term strategy hat and envision for yourself a future that will enrich and empower your life and those you care about. If you wish, sketch out an Objectives Tree with your Vision at the top, as this *Star Trek* fan did in Figure 12.1.

Reading down from the top shows How
Reading up from the bottom shows Why

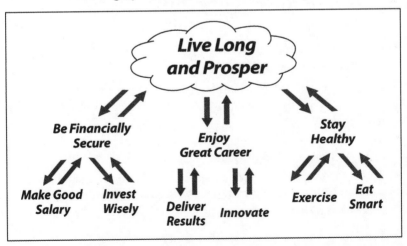

FIGURE 12.1   Personal Objectives Tree Example

To stimulate your own ideas, below are some life categories with sample goal statements and project examples under each. Some of these are big projects that warrant a LogFrame. Others may be considered more like tasks, habits or ways of being.

As you read through these examples, highlight a few that intrigue you, and let them trigger fresh ideas of your own.

Career

To experience a productive, profitable, and satisfying career that enables me to do work that matters with people who care.

- Learning new skills through virtual training, in-person courses, and practice
- Increasing my online/social media visibility and credibility
- Getting a professional certification or completing an advanced degree
- Taking on a new role at my workplace
- Creating satisfying relationships with my manager and co-workers
- Earning a raise or promotion at my current organization
- Finding a mentor and being one to others

Finances

To prosper by earning and managing my finances in a way that fulfills all of my commitments and creates security for my family.

- Developing a budget and sticking to it
- Investing in rental properties
- Starting, growing, or selling a business
- Creating a new income source
- Reducing frivolous spending
- Creating a long-term financial retirement plan

Family/Relationship/Social Life

To create close, mutually supportive, enriching, and caring relationships with family and friends.

- Finding a new partner who shares my values
- Planning a wedding

- Raising a loving and supportive family
- Playing games with my children we both enjoy
- Planning an exciting experience, with friends or family
- Making all my relationships more fulfilling, joyful, and fun
- Being a great parent, grandparent, son or daughter, brother or sister
- Reconnecting with long-lost friends

Community

To experience connection and fulfillment while being an active contributor to the people, causes, and communities that matter to me.

- Expanding my social network (friends, professional groups, on-line contacts)
- Becoming a Big Brother or Big Sister to help children in my community
- Joining others in a project that helps solve a social, health, or environmental problem
- Volunteering on a project that brings me satisfaction while making a difference for others
- Organizing a community garden
- Collecting toys for children who do not have many toys
- Running for political office or campaigning for a political candidate

Personal Development/Self-Mastery

To learn and grow in all dimensions of my life, to develop and use all my unique gifts and be an inspiration to others.

- Attending an in-depth growth workshop led by a master teacher
- Reading the biographies of my role models
- Expanding my comfort zone by taking an exhilarating risk (e.g., barefoot fire-walking)
- Creating a group of growth-minded people who support each other
- Letting go of my limiting beliefs, habits, and assumptions
- Adding positive daily practices that bring value to my life now
- Developing greater confidence and resilience by mindfully managing my thoughts and emotions

Health/Fitness

To experience vibrant health and emotional well-being by taking consistent actions to nourish, strengthen, and take care of my body for a long, healthy, and energized life.

- Improving physical health and mental stamina
- Consistently exercising and lowering my Body Mass Index
- Training for a 5K or marathon
- Taking an online yoga, dance, fitness, or martial arts class
- Eating healthy foods consistently (while enjoying some desserts in moderation)
- Leading an outdoor adventure

Learning and Skill Development

To be a lifelong learner on topics of interest to me, both professionally and personally, and to stay informed about broader global issues.

- Embarking on a learning journey in a new field
- Becoming an expert authority in my field
- Learning to speak another language
- Writing thoughtful articles or a book, or creating artwork
- Learning to tell stories in a way that moves people emotionally
- Learning to play a musical instrument
- Improving reading speed, accuracy, and retention

Spiritual Life/Emotional Expression

To stay connected to myself and a higher power through prayers, meditation, and reading inspirational materials that reinforce my Vision while keeping me calm and grounded.

- Meditating consistently to become more mindful
- Participating in spiritual events with music
- Taking on a simple practice, such as expressing gratitude daily
- Forgiving myself and others and reclaiming stuck energy
- Reconnecting with source
- Creating or joining a growth-oriented mastermind group
- Acknowledging people for their contribution to me while they are still living

Work Space/Living Space

To maintain stylish, comfortable, and inspiring living spaces that support my professional commitments and personal enjoyment.

- Creating an efficient, attractive, and ergonomic home office
- Cleaning out an overstuffed garage, closet, or files
- Decorating my living space with art that enlivens my spirit
- Remodeling or repainting selected parts of my house
- Landscaping a backyard into an oasis retreat
- Keeping my files, books, and belongings organized and tidy

Hobbies/Fun/Recreation/Adventure

To build fun, play, excitement, and whimsy into my life on my own and with others.

- Enjoying high play and adventures with my best friends
- Teaming with my "best dog friend" in an agility obstacle course
- Turning my hobby into an online business
- Rediscovering and enjoying a hobby from my youth
- Identifying and documenting 100 species of birds
- Organizing a scavenger hunt or game day

Which ones caught your eye? What ideas did this generate for you? Which possibilities intrigue you? Which ones would bring greater richness and variety into your life? Which ones are compelling enough to act on?

While some people only dream about their desired future, others get busy creating it. Permit me to challenge you to commit to yourself to move forward on one or more of your project ideas. Start by taking an item from your "someday" list and turn it into an "action now" or "today" list item. Build it out into a LogFrame project plan and move into action.

Commit Yourself to Make It Happen

Now that you've identified the project topics you're energized about pursuing, you're ready to make it happen.

Step 3: Design Your Priority Projects

Start by doing this: Choose one of the examples described above or craft your own. Write this Objective on a blank sheet of paper. Then draw an upward arrow that points to the *Why*, and a downward arrow that points to *How*. Then write one or more Objectives in each direction.

You can expand this into an Objectives Tree if you wish. Just make sure it hangs together in a causal fashion. Then, just as we did with the Asian gypsy moth example in Chapter 7, you can move elements of your Objectives Tree into the Logical Framework matrix.

Assumptions play an especially powerful role in personal projects, because they deal with your core values and beliefs. The Assumptions you make about yourself and the mindset you bring will determine if you even take the first step toward these goals. If you choose to assume and believe that you are capable and worthy, you will take action to make it real. If not, you may not even try.

But as you begin to move forward in a new direction, your inner critic will raise its negative voice and find ways to resist. It will tell you it is not worth it . . . it won't work anyway . . . why even bother . . . who you ?. . . get serious! The more ambitious the intended change, the further these steps are outside your comfort zone, the louder this critic becomes. Learn to defeat the critic by tuning in to your inner cheerleader and practice positive internal messaging.

Step 4: Take Imperfect Action

Get a blank calendar and put a check on each day you act on your life project. Using a calendar is important because what gets scheduled usually gets done. Keep a journal and write down daily at least one step in the direction of achieving your Vision. You will be amazed at the progress you make through these basic practices.

Start simple. To get into momentum quickly and avoid becoming overwhelmed, I recommend working on not more than three personal projects at a time. The bonus materials include several fully-developed personal project LogFrames that serve as examples.

Break big chunks down into bite size steps, and each day perform an action that moves you forward. If you have a "perfection complex," or find yourself procrastinating, muster up the courage to take action steps every day anyway. Procrastination is a symptom of a fear of failure or a sense of being undeserving. The very best way to bust that fear is to take uncomfortable, imperfect, forward-focused action.

When working on ambitious goals, do not expect you will "get it right," much less perfect, as you proceed. Experiment with different behaviors and approaches. See what works. Fail. Learn. Improve. Remember that life is a work in progress and let your approach be adaptive, not prescriptive.

The most common excuse for not taking action on goals you say you want is lack of time. Just realize that time is seldom the real reason; the real reason is a lack of priority and sense of importance. You just have to decide whether you are going to make yourself a priority. Carving out just 15 minutes daily to work on your life projects amounts to over 90 hours a year. That's plenty of time to accomplish something significant.

Imagine for a moment you are 99 years old, sitting in your rocking chair, looking back on your life. Will you feel content and satisfied? Or will you feel disappointed and regret over the opportunities not seized, the chances not taken, the full expression of life you could have experienced but did not. The pain of regret cuts deep, and someday it will be too late. Your time to *go for it* and live your fullest is *now*.

Step 5: Review, Replan, and Recommit

The three types of assessment described in Chapter 9—Monitor, Review, and Evaluate—will keep you on track.

Each day, *monitor* the steps you take towards your goals. Aim to take one or more actions that move you closer to your envisioned future each day. Put it on your daily agenda because when a task is scheduled, it gets done. Also, get a blank calendar and put a check mark (or a gold star) for each day you act on your project. Not all projects are suited to daily action; some require dedicated blocks of time during a week. Review your results weekly, and give yourself a "score." You will be amazed at the progress you make through this simple habit.

From time to time, perhaps quarterly, *review*. Start with a *personal strategy refresh* to examine the progress made on the projects you have on your radar. Cross off the ones you have reached or want to let go. If there are Goals you set but took no action toward, ask why. Do an honest evaluation and decide whether to recommit or drop them. Here are some valid reasons to remove goals and/or projects from your list:

1. The opportunity window has closed.
2. They are someone else's goals for you but not yours.
3. You have evolved and that goal no longer serves you.
4. There are more compelling goals you want to pursue now.
5. You have accomplished the goal intention in another way.

Annually, *evaluate*. Review the current external conditions and your personal circumstances. What has changed in your environment? Take a broader look at where you are now and where you want to be; then set new more appropriate goals. Doing this on your birthday each year is the best gift you can give yourself.

Visualize your future-self experiencing the benefits of each goal to stay motivated. Your goals need not be earth-shattering or world-changing. They just need to be yours.

Manage Your Dreams and Disappointments

Not all of the goals you most desire will be realized. Do not feel guilt, shame, or blame if they do not happen as you mapped them out. If you took no action, this usually means that the ghoal was not a high enough priority. Or perhaps you were not ready, or life got in the way. Maybe the uncontrollable factors in the outside environment did not cooperate. In any event, extract the learning. The lessons of those unrealized goals may help you be successful with another goal that matters to you even more.

Reframing Disappointment and Failure

In the opening chapters of this book I recounted the story of my early life dreams of becoming a Rocket Man. But that dream never happened. I did not follow a career in the aerospace industry, become an astronaut, or visit the moon myself. Some might say I failed at that life goal. But that's not how I framed it. I consider that goal as accomplished, but not in the way I anticipated.

My career as a strategy coach, consultant, and trainer has supported many other people, institutions, companies, and even countries in rocketing their goals ahead by launching successful projects. Nothing could be more satisfying and rewarding to me than being able to connect with and empower so many other amazing people who have hopes and dreams; and doing it one client, student, or reader at a time.

So, in my mind and heart, I am still in the "rocket business," just in a different way. My business is to launch *you*!

The larger life lesson I learned from my experience is this: Behind every goal there rests a deeper motivation connected to one's foundational core values and Vision. In my case, it was not the smell of rocket fuel that attracted me. Rather, it was the challenge of doing something significant and contributing to something meaningful. In hindsight, I have no regrets because so many other opportunities and life paths opened up that I would not have seen otherwise. Just as many roads lead to Rome, there are multiple paths to fulfill any core desire.

When you have a big goal, you expand yourself in the process of moving towards it, whether or not you reach it. The mental and emotional muscles you acquire in goal-setting and goal-getting increase your capacity to seize even greater opportunities as they present themselves, once you are prepared to take them on.

Deep in each of us stirs a longing to be significant and know our life has meaning. Remember that the principles in this book, while focused on "work projects," apply just as well to the unique projects that make up your life journey. You have the opportunity to be fulfilling your Vision right now, today, contributing your gifts to others, and experiencing profound fulfillment. Enjoy the journey. Celebrate your own success and that of others.

Be Grateful for It All

Be grateful for all you have experienced, including the mistakes and setbacks. Reframe them as learning opportunities. What qualities did you gain from your difficult experiences? Was it compassion, resilience, or courage? Did you become wiser? Be thankful for all the mistakes you made because they taught you life lessons. Be grateful for all the obstacles you overcame because you grew stronger. And if you find yourself going through hell, keep going!

I am grateful for the rich and varied path I have been able to follow, despite plenty of failures and disappointment along the way. My path has taken me from being an engineer to a strategic planner; project manager to international development advisor and political campaign manager; project manager to coach, consultant, author, and university instructor, as well as being a good father, a good husband, a good friend, and a force for good in the world.

Not reaching my Rocket Man goal has enabled me to do what's much more fulfilling and important: adding to the lives of others.

Project Yourself into the Future

We have used the words *project* and *projects* as a noun 782 times in this book. But this word can also be a verb, meaning to *project* yourself forward into the future each of us is intentionally creating. You are creating that future *today* with your projects, your declarations, your self-expression, and your active collaboration with others. Being the best version of you is strategy at its best.

By putting into action the lessons and strategic principles woven into the preceding chapters, you can reap long-term benefits—no matter who you are. I would love to hear how you are using this approach in your work or personal projects. Drop me an email at the address shown after this chapter.

My ultimate aim in writing this book has been to give you the tools and inspiration you need to live a magnificent life. Now it is up to you. Implement what you learned and you will move big mountains more quickly. People who can do that are both rare and urgently needed, and now you are one of them.

Review Key Points

1. Your most essential projects concern your life. The principles we have covered apply equally well to your professional and personal projects.
2. Strategic *Life* Management is really all about: envisioning the life you want; being the person you want to be, and making the impact you want to make.

3. Give yourself the gift of clarity. Annually, on your birthday, do a deep dive into your Vision, values, and goals.

4. Keep your Purpose fresh by writing it in bold colors and taping it to your wall or mirror, and share it with friends, family, and associates. Keep a journal and write down daily at least one step you took in the direction of achieving your Purpose/Vision.

5. Create a simple life project portfolio, perhaps starting with an Objectives Tree. Identify a variety of ways you can move toward your Vision. Keep your goals fluid, and break them down into smaller chunks you can work on daily.

6. Realize that not all of your goals will be realized; do not blame yourself or others if they do not happen. As you progress, some goals may become obsolete or no longer inspire you. Just let them go and create something more compelling!

7. Choose at least one project to put into action in the next ten days. LogFrame it! Then do it!

Coming Up Next

You have now completed all 12 chapters of this book. I trust that you find these tools to be not only useful but empowering, and will apply them to your work projects and to the most essential project, which is you and your life.

The next chapter is yours to write. What will you do with what you have learned? What new ideas will you initiate? What bigger challenges are you willing to take on? How will you engage with your teams differently? How will you continue to build your confidence and resilience to optimize the power of you?

The story of how you will do that is your chapter to write. The great news is you now have the tools and skills and insights you need to create a fresh path in front of you. That untrodden path invites you to start walking on it today and to leave your footprints. That's how you are going to write your chapter.

I cannot wait to read it.

We Are Here to Support You

If you want to deepen your strategic skills or get your projects off to a smooth and fast start, we are here to assist you with customized training and coaching. We support individuals, teams, and special task forces by video conferencing as well as on site delivery; Terry and his team are committed to your success and can help you to:

- **Sharpen Your Strategic Plans.** Get expert guidance in applying the eight-step "Quick and Clean" strategic refresh process to improve or pivot your organization.
- **Assist with Project Design.** We can work directly with you to build strong teams and design winning projects.
- **Review Draft LogFrames.** Get a comprehensive review of draft designs you create, and receive specific improvement suggestions.
- **Train Your Team.** Train your entire team in best practices to achieve shared understanding and jump-start project execution.
- **Develop Strategic Mastery.** Learn advanced LogFrame and other strategic tools at your convenience in a robust and flexible online environment.
- **Train Your Trainers.** Equip your own trainers to teach project teams and facilitate project design. Create a self-sufficient delivery capability and get all of our teaching material.

Claim Your Free Book Bonus Materials—Quick Start Pack. This includes project designs you can model, our seven-step strategy refresh process, the LogFrame quality checklist, plus additional resources to help you implement projects with greater ease. There is no obligation, this is simply my way to thank you for purchasing this book. Available at www.ManagementPro.com/bookbonus.

Additionally, each month, we offer a limited number of complimentary strategy sessions. Please use the following link to apply for a session to discuss ways to bring your projects and strategies to life: www.ManagementPro.com/strategysession.

Finally, if you have questions about anything in this book, your project, or our services, or just want to connect, I'd love to hear from you. You can email me at StrategicTerry@ManagementPro.com.

Here are other ways we can connect:

Linked In: https://www.linkedin.com/in/terryschmidt/
Twitter: https://twitter.com/StrategicTerry
YouTube: https://www.youtube.com/user/terrydeanschmidt

Thank you again. I look forward to hearing how *Strategic Project Management* is making a difference for you.

Glossary and Usage of Terms

Activities The action steps or tasks to be undertaken to produce Outcomes.

Assumptions External factors that influence project success over which the project manager has no direct control. Assumptions can be monitored, influenced, and sometimes managed.

Baseline data Data describing the conditions when a project is started. Provides a basis to determine the nature and extent of change caused by the project.

Bottom-up Begin at the Input level and use *If-Then* thinking to logically link Outcomes, Purpose, and Goal. Bottom-up thinking can test the causal logic of a strategy and validate top-down planning.

Chunking The process of logically breaking down something large into smaller parts.

Chunking logic Criteria chosen for organizing project elements (e.g., phase, function, discipline, process, milestones).

Coupling Situations in which one project element affects or depends on an element from another project. These dependencies or impacts can be recognized in the Assumptions column.

Disaggregation Breaking down a large or complex Objective into smaller components.

End of project status (EOPS) The set of Success Measures that identify achievement of the project's Purpose.

Evaluation An orderly examination of progress at each level of Objective using fact-based evidence. Establishes the validity of hypotheses in order to improve the current project and learn lessons for future projects. Evaluation examines the

Outcome-Purpose-Goal linkages, while monitoring examines the Input-Output linkage.

Execution Moving plans into action and achieving project Objectives. Also called implementation.

Gantt chart Also called a bar chart, this graphic tool is for scheduling and monitoring project tasks and activities. Gantt charts display key activities vertically and activity duration estimates horizontally.

Goal The higher-level, broader, strategic, or program Objective immediately above project Purpose.

Horizontal logic A term that expresses the combination of Objectives, Success Measures, and Means of Verification at each level in the LogFrame.

Hypothesis An educated guess; a predictive statement about a causal relationship involving uncertainty. The predicted and intended means-end relationship between each level in the LogFrame constitutes a set of linked *If-Then* hypotheses.

***If-Then* thinking** A way to express cause-effect, means-ends relationships as a series of "if-this, then-that" statements.

Indicators Part of Success Measures. Indicators are targets with numerical description of quantity, quality (performance), time, cost, and client/customer.

Inputs Activities and resources (time, money, and people) needed to produce Outcomes.

Leading indicators Future-focused Success Measures that can be observable now, used to predict the future status of Objectives.

Linked hypotheses A connected series of predicted *If-Then* statements about project relationships. These can appear in the Objectives column of the LogFrame and in Objectives trees.

Logical Framework (LogFrame) A set of interlocking concepts organized into a 4x4 matrix for logically designing sound project strategy.

Manageable interest Identifies the portion of a larger enterprise believed to be achievable, and defines the responsibility of the Project Leader. The Project Leader commits to produce Outcomes by effectively managing the activities, given appropriate levels of resources. It is in their manageable interest to modify activities and do whatever is necessary to produce Outcomes.

Matrix for the Logical Framework   A 4×4 matrix that displays the interrelationships of components of a project. The matrix is divided into four *rows* (for Goal, Purpose, Outcomes, and Inputs) and four *columns* (for Objectives, Success Measures, Verification, and Assumptions).

Means of Verification   The source and means of obtaining data used to verify an indicator or Measure (e.g., market share as determined by the marketing department).

Monitoring   The management function of following the progress and overseeing the operations of a project. Monitoring focuses on the Input-to-Outcome linkage of the LogFrame.

Objective   A desired project result or intention. These are further distinguished as Outcomes, Purpose, Goal, Super Goal, or Vision. (Note that Inputs are actions toward Objectives, but are not an Objective.)

Objectives Tree   A visual tool using *If-Then* logic to clarify relationships among Objectives in complex environments and to compare alternative approaches to reach the Goals.

Outcomes   The results believed to be necessary and sufficient to achieve the project's Purpose.

Outputs   A term sometimes used in general project management to express what we call Outcomes.

PFA   Acronym for "plucked from air." In other words, a guess not backed by evidence.

Program   A "strategy" consisting of groups of projects all contributing to the same Goal. A *Program* is managed to achieve a Goal, just as a *Project* is managed to achieve a Purpose.

Project   Classic definition: An organized system of interrelated activities and processes established to achieve specified Objectives on time and within budget. Schmidt definition: Engines of progress and change.

Project design A summary of what the project is expected to achieve (Goal and Purpose), what it must deliver to achieve Purpose (Outcomes), and how it will deliver Outcomes (Inputs). The key elements of a project design may be summarized in the Logical Framework format.

Project Leader The person who accepts responsibility for producing Outcomes that achieve Purpose, given necessary Inputs.

Purpose What is hoped to be achieved by undertaking the project. Purpose describes the anticipated change in behavior or system conditions expected when the required Outcomes are produced.

RAP (Rapid Action Planning) session Focused workshops that build key executable action plans with a core team quickly, while establishing good team norms.

Psychological safety Being able to be and act as one's own self without fear of negative consequences. A belief the team is safe for interpersonal risk taking.

Scientific method A process for formulating a hypothesis and testing its validity through experimentation.

Strategic Action cycle A systems perspective of a project that considers the three distinct phases of a project (design, implementation, and evaluation) or (think, plan, act, and assess) as an integrated system.

Strategic hypothesis Represents a prediction that *If* the expected results at one level of the LogFrame hierarchy are achieved, and *If* the Assumptions at that level are valid, *Then* the expected results at the next higher level will be achieved.

Strategy An organized set of programs, projects, and initiatives undertaken to achieve the organization's Vision.

Success Measures The target(s) for an Objective that indicates it has been achieved. Targets can include quantity, quality, time frame, customer, and cost. Measures established during the design phase of a project provide the basis for subsequent monitoring and evaluation.

SWAG Acronym for the term "Scientific Wild-Ass Guess," a rough estimate made by an expert in the field, based on experience and intuition. Considered more scientific than a WAG, an off-the-cuff estimate based on limited data or experience. Not to be confused with a less accurate guestimation technique known as PFA (Plucked from Air).

System   A set of interrelated elements that work together to reach the overall Objectives. Systems are sometimes described as a strategy or process for producing Outcomes and achieving Purpose from given Inputs.

Systems thinking   A broad-based, wide-angle holistic view that situates projects within the larger context in which they operate.

Top-down   Planning that proceeds from the general to the particular, or from the broad to the detailed. In the LogFrame, this begins with Goal and Purpose, then proceeds to Outcomes and Inputs.

Vertical logic   A way to summarize the *If-Then* linkages among Objectives.

Work breakdown structure   Tool for disaggregating a system or Objective into component parts. Each Outcome is broken down into smaller components. The process continues to develop logical work packages that can be costed, scheduled, assigned, and implemented.

About the Author

Terry Schmidt believes project leaders are the unsung superheroes of our time. His mission is to help them become more purposeful, productive, powerful, and profitable. He brings four decades of experience as a strategist, educator, and consultant who has assisted corporations, governments, nonprofits, and research institutions in 42 countries worldwide.

His work with leaders at the highest levels of organizations worldwide has cemented his reputation as a strategic thinker and "rockstar" facilitator reaching over 25,000 professionals.

Terry is the founder and president of Seattle-based ManagementPro.com, a management consulting firm. A master consultant, Terry has helped hundreds of organizations of all types to successfully turn strategic ideas into committed action and quality results. Teams transformed by Terry's work include Apple Inc., Blizzard Entertainment, Symantec, eBay, Boeing, Moog, Sony Electronics, Walt Disney Imagineering, DirecTV, Northrop-Grumman, the Los Angeles Department of Water and Power, Thai Airways, the Federal Reserve Board, the U.S. Department of Energy, and the National Research Laboratories (Sandia, Lawrence Livermore, Los Alamos, and Pacific National).

He provides on-site and virtual services to help clients sharpen their strategies and smoothly turn them into successful projects. In addition to his consulting practices Terry is an award-winning faculty member at leading universities and international executive management programs, including The Institute for Management Studies, the MIT Professional Institute, and the UCLA Extension Technical Management Program.

Terry earned an MBA from Harvard University. Prior to that, he graduated from the University of Washington with a BS in aerospace engineering. He has been certified as a Strategic Management

211

Professional (SPM) by the Association for Strategic Planning (ASP), and a Project Management Professional (PMP) by the Project Management Institute (PMI). Terry served as an advisor on the national task force that developed competency standards for certifying strategic planners. He is a popular keynote speaker at conferences and has written seven books on business strategy, career/life strategy, and peak performance.

Terry brings creativity, passion, and a multidisciplinary system thinking approach that his clients appreciate. His training programs and custom facilitation sessions have a reputation for being lively, innovative, and producing solid results.

When he is not working, Terry enjoys reading, cracking jokes to anyone who will listen, and cruising around the neighborhood on his electric bike with his dog Rufus chasing him.

Index